Elite • 246

Gladiators
4th–1st centuries BC

FRANÇOIS GILBERT

ILLUSTRATED BY GIUSEPPE RAVA
Series editors Martin Windrow & Nick Reynolds

OSPREY PUBLISHING
Bloomsbury Publishing Plc
Kemp House, Chawley Park, Cumnor Hill, Oxford OX2 9PH, UK
29 Earlsfort Terrace, Dublin 2, Ireland
1385 Broadway, 5th Floor, New York, NY 10018, USA
E-mail: info@ospreypublishing.com
www.ospreypublishing.com

OSPREY is a trademark of Osprey Publishing Ltd

First published in Great Britain in 2022

A catalogue record for this book is available from the British Library.

ISBN: PB 9781472850928; eBook 9781472850904;
ePDF 9781472850881; XML 9781472850874

22 23 24 25 26   10 9 8 7 6 5 4 3 2 1

Index by Rob Munro
Typeset by PDQ Digital Media Solutions, Bungay, UK
Printed and bound in India by Replika Press Private Ltd.

To find out more about our authors and books visit
www.ospreypublishing.com. Here you will find extracts, author
interviews, details of forthcoming events and the option to sign up for our
newsletter.

Acknowledgements

First and foremost, I would like to thank Nick Reynolds and Martin Windrow
for their trust in me. Without them, this book would not have been
possible. I also thank my great friend Raffaele D'Amato, who is a great
scholar, and who knows how to constantly renew our vision of Antiquity.
He gave me the benefit of his incredible photo library, and his connections
in many European museums to complete the iconography of this work.
Through him, may all these museums be thanked. My special thanks also to
the Musée Lugdunum in Lyon, France, and the Royal Ontario Museum in
Toronto, Canada, for their invaluable assistance. I don't forget all my friends,
who for years have visited many sites and museums to bring me new
images. Thanks to Noémie Ledouble, Gilles Habasque, Olaf and Bernd
Kueppers, Damien Bouet, Stéphane Lagrange and Michel Gilbert.

Artist's note

Readers may care to note that the original paintings from which the colour
plates in this book were prepared are available for private sale. All
reproduction copyright whatsoever is retained by the publishers. All
enquiries should be addressed to:

info@g-rava.it

The publishers regret that they can enter into no correspondence upon
this matter.

Front cover, above: The amphitheatre of Pompeii. Like football today,
gladiatorialism ignited the passions of the ancient Romans. The similarities
between the two are many: both are sports governed by rules and
overseen by referees; they have their 'stars', whose images are displayed on
many derivative products; and they generate a vast economy supporting
thousands of people in a wide variety of professions. In Rome,
gladiatorialism was an important foundation for the stability of the Empire.
That was not the case in its early days, however. (Author)

Title-page illustration: A funeral duel in the 4th century BC. This depiction is
held at the Museo archeologico nazionale di Paestum (Capaccio Paestum,
Italy). (R. D'Amato)

CONTENTS

GLADIATORS
4TH–1ST CENTURIES BC

ORIGINS AND EVOLUTION

Dated to *c*.390–380 BC, the earliest images of 'spectacle fights' come from the regions of Campania and Lucania in southern Italy. Scenes painted on the walls of tombs in Capua, Albanella, Altavilla Silentina and especially at Paestum actually represent funeral games, organized to honour the memory of the deceased. We see chariot races, boxing fights, running and javelin throwing, but also duels with weapons. These scenes are not meant to depict sham clashes, because blood is flowing from the fighters' wounds; this blood was believed to permeate the earth and nourish the soul of the deceased. The fighters (we cannot yet call them 'gladiators') were normally illustrious men, friends or relatives of the deceased. Although the fight was meant to stop at the 'first blood' (*vulneribus tenu*), it was sometimes difficult for these elite warriors to control themselves, as the adrenaline and the desire for prestige kept them fighting.

To satisfy the dead with a bloody offering, human sacrifices of captives or slaves were also carried out. Such scenes are depicted in ancient art, for example in the François Tomb (Vulci, Italy). To replace the duels between families of the deceased, it was decided to make such captives fight among themselves, which gave one of them a chance to survive (Tertullian, *De Spectaculis* XII.2–3; see also Servius, *Ad Aeneid* X.519). The victory was granted to the fighter's master, and not to the fighter himself (Pliny the Elder, *Naturalis Historia* XXI.5). Because they fought in front of funeral pyres, these men were called *bustuarii* (from *bustum*, 'pyre'). This term is cited only by Cicero (*In Pisonem* IX.19) and Servius (*Ad Aen.* X.519), however, who drew upon earlier sources. We can see in this development the beginnings of the 'professionalization' of gladiatorialism.

Funeral combat (left) and chariot racing (right) are shown in this depiction, dating from the 4th century BC and held at the Museo archeologico nazionale di Paestum (Capaccio Paestum, Italy). (R. D'Amato)

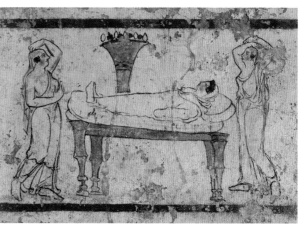

ABOVE LEFT
Boxing, accompanied by music, at the funeral of a rich Campanian. This depiction is held at the Museo archeologico nazionale di Paestum. (R. D'Amato)

ABOVE RIGHT
A funeral scene in Campania, 4th century BC; the dead man is surrounded by mourners. This depiction is held at the Museo archeologico nazionale di Paestum. (R. D'Amato)

One theory, propounded in antiquity by Nicolaus of Damascus and recounted by Athenaeus of Naucratis (*Deipnosophistae* IV.153f), was that the Etruscans were the inventors of gladiatorialism. In reality, the Etruscans inherited it from the Campanians, at the end of the 4th or the beginning of the 3rd century BC, and then passed it on to the Romans, who organized the first known combat in 264 BC (Valerius Maximus, *Factorum ac dictorum memorabilium libri IX* II.4.7; Livy, *Ab Urbe Condita* XVI). Under the influence of Rome, gladiatorialism spread in the 2nd century BC throughout and then beyond the Italian peninsula. This was particularly the case in Spain, where in 206 BC Scipio gave a memorable show in Cartagena, in memory of his late father and uncle. Gladiatorialism was also found in Syria in 167 BC, with the Seleucid king Antiochos IV Epiphanes (r. 175–164 BC) having no fewer than 240 pairs of gladiators pitted against each other. While Etruscan gladiatorialism faded towards the end of the 2nd century BC, Roman gladiatorism, on the contrary, experienced a surge in interest and innovation that would know no bounds for five centuries.

At first the audience for such combats was still restricted to the family circles of the deceased. In view of the general enthusiasm for these bloody battles, however, in 105 BC the consuls decided to invite all Romans to attend. These were now shows (*munera*) offered to the people to divert and distract them; the memory of the dead was no more than a pretext. Other reasons now existed: dedication of a monument, anniversary, military victory, thanksgiving, etc. The elites of Italy, and later other Roman provinces, offered increasing numbers of ever more elaborate shows. In the first documented combat, in 264 BC, three pairs of gladiators fought; there were 22 pairs in 216 BC, then 50 pairs in 183 BC. The final years of the Republic saw the golden age of the *munera*.

Three eras of gladiatorialism

Ancient writers wrote a great deal about gladiatorialism, but sadly left us no comprehensive study or history of it. We only have disparate anecdotes or information, and those are very fragmentary. We do have an abundant iconography – mosaics, oil-lamp medallions, bas-reliefs, graffiti, figurines, etc. – but unfortunately, this *corpus* is very incomplete for the 3rd and 2nd centuries BC. These sources can be assembled to help us better understand gladiators' lives and deaths. The images also tell us about the very specific equipment of these fighters; and they are supplemented by some rare

The execution of prisoners – a common scene in Italic art. This depiction is housed at the Museo Etrusco Guarnacci (Volterra, Italy). (R. D'Amato)

BELOW LEFT
In this depiction of a duel between *essedarii* or *Galli*, held at the Römisch-Germanisches Museum (Cologne, Germany), the vanquished has raised his finger to ask for his pardon. (B. Kueppers)

BELOW RIGHT
Depicted in a relief at Benevento (Italy), a defeated *hoplomachus* places his *mirmillo* opponent's dagger in the optimal spot, thus making the kill painless. (Author's drawing)

archaeological artefacts. All this information enables us to identify the different categories of gladiators (*armaturae*), which became very codified. Thus, spectators immediately recognized the gladiators who entered the arena, and could distinguish a *Thraex*, a *mirmillo* (alternatively *myrmillo* or *murmillo*), a *Samnis* or a *retiarius*. For convenience, we can divide the first centuries of gladiatorialism into three periods, each of which corresponds to profound changes.

The first period is that of its Campanian origins. It begins at the start of the 4th century BC, possibly before, and ends in 310 BC, when the Samnites were defeated by the Romans and their Campanian allies. This date corresponds to a famous text by Livy (*Ab Urbe Condita* IX.40) that evokes the birth of the first true 'gladiators', after this event. In reality, Livy's text was an attempt – revealed by several anachronisms – to explain *a posteriori* (reasoning from observed facts) the *armatura* of the *Samnis*. Livy recounts, in fact, that after their victory, the Campanians recovered enemy weapons on the battlefield, and then gave them to prisoners of war, who were forced to fight during banquets. This archaic gladiatorialism was still only a regional phenomenon, however. During this period, the fighters clashed using local weapons and fighting techniques, mainly the spear or javelin and the round shield. We cannot yet speak of gladiatorialism, nor of gladiators; but at the end of this period, for the first time, a ritual duel intended to honour a deceased person was desacralized and presented as entertainment.

In the 3rd century BC began the 'ethnic' period, so called because it concerned other populations. Funerary gladiatorialism was then exported from Campania to the Etruscans. It was probably at this time that the first distinctions between combatants were created, due to the use of different weaponry, in order to provide variety. Up until then, there were only combatants armed like *Samnites*. In the 3rd century BC, the enemies of the Etruscans were the Gauls. This was why a category of Gallic gladiators – *Galli* – appeared, who used their ethnic weaponry. The Etruscans also had another enemy at the time: the Romans. It is therefore probable that they also invented an *armatura* of the *Romani*, later abandoned after the latter's military victory. This is only a hypothesis, but a reasonable one.

The 'ethnic' phase lasted until the Spartacus revolt (73–71 BC). In the meantime, new *armaturae* were created. The number of gladiator categories (at least those that would remain and of which we are aware) was ultimately very low, which is surprising, because gladiatorialism had already existed for more than three centuries. The explanation is arguably simple: not all captured enemies could be transformed into effective gladiators who could fight singly. Most prisoners of war were used to fighting in formation. In other words, the ethnic gladiatorial system contained within itself its own limitations, imposed by the scarcity of adversaries who could offer audience the spectacle of single combat. It is possible that there were other attempts: a hypothetical Carthaginian *armatura*, or that of the Germans (Sallust, *Historiae* CCCXXXVII). Only the most interesting and promising must have survived.

A third period, that of 'technical' gladiatorialism, is easier to date, because it corresponded to a profound change imposed by the Spartacus revolt. After this rebellion, the Romans realized that it was no longer wise to concentrate in schools (*ludi*) men who lived in slavery because of the Romans, and to make them experts in killing. From then on, it became obvious that it was necessary to vary the recruitment channels. If gladiatorialism was to last, the system had to change. While it continued to use many prisoners and convicts, gladiatorialism was now also open to volunteers: free men and freed men, but also slaves who wanted a career. It was therefore no longer possible for the vanquished to be put to death, otherwise there would be no more candidates. The authorities then imagined different levels of fighting, more or less dangerous, with rewards for the winners, in order to create emulation. Fighting to the death became the exception at the beginning of the Principate, as gladiatorialism evolved and became a sport.

Gladiators could also be hired for hunts (*venationes*). In this depiction from the Collezione Torlonia (Palazzo Orsini, Rome, Italy), we see two *mirmillones*, one *eques* on the ground, and two *Thraeces* who have exchanged their *sicae* for straight swords, which were more useful for fighting animals. (Author's drawing)

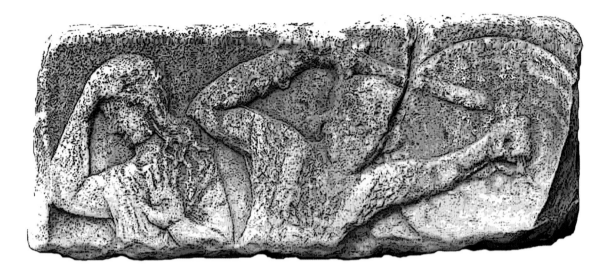

In this bas-relief from Civitella San Paolo (Italy), dating from the end of the 1st century BC, an *eques* (right) is equipped with a scale breastplate with leather shoulder pads. A grieving woman (left) suggests the funereal context. (Author's drawing)

In the 1st century BC, ambitious Romans such as Catiline, Clodius and Caesar formed troops of gladiators, ostensibly in order to entertain the masses but in practice to gain political leverage. After his victory at the naval battle of Actium (31 BC), Octavian (known as Augustus from the start of his reign as emperor in 27 BC) changed the system to his own advantage, to prevent any competition. He initiated great reforms in 22 BC, arrogating to himself a virtual monopoly on big shows in the capital. The shows were now carried out with the express authorization of the state, which imposed certain limitations (only 120 pairs of gladiators for the magistrates' games, for example). The emperor's own spectacles were not affected by these limitations, however, and were of extreme munificence.

At the start of the Principate, the shows systematically combined gladiatorial fights (held during the afternoon) with hunts (*venationes*) during the morning, public executions at the midday (*meridiani*) break and other spectacular acts. To provide variety and spectacle, other *armaturae* were introduced, sometimes based upon old categories that evolved. Unlike the previous ones, however, these new categories no longer concerned defeated peoples; some even had nothing to do with the military. This 'technical' gladiatorialism would last until the end of the 2nd century AD.

In this depiction held at the Museo archeologico nazionale di Paestum, two warriors fight under the supervision of a referee, who holds the crown to be awarded to the victor. From the outset, referees watched the fights, and intervened when necessary, as in any athletic competition. The referees were recognizable by their long, straight, flexible stick, and their gestures were codified. The fights also took place against a background of music, provided by trumpet players. (R. D'Amato)

This frieze depicting gladiatorial equipment is held at the Musée lapidaire de Narbonne (France). Probably in conjunction with the instructors (*doctores*) and the doctor (*medicus*), the *lanista* decided the assignments in a particular category of combatants. For this, the recruit must have undergone a medical examination and physical tests. His size was naturally taken into account, and those who showed exceptional dispositions could even be entered in more than one category. Left-handed (*scaevae*) and ambidextrous (*aequimani*) gladiators were also identified. While the *auctorati* might have had a say in the choice of their speciality, some owners of *familia gladiatoria* paid little attention to a reasoned assignment of their recruits, and simply had them draw lots for their *armatura*, as Cicero testifies (*Pro Sest.* LXIV.134). (R. D'Amato)

BECOMING A GLADIATOR

The famous warriors who fought the first funeral battles illustrating the tombs of Campania and Lucania were soon replaced by slaves or condemned men, whose lives were considered to be worthless. To fuel these bloody exhibitions, the Campanians, then the Etruscans and the Romans, logically preferred

A *Gallus* executes his opponent by thrusting the point of his sword into the base of the neck, causing an instant and almost painless death. This depiction is held at the Antiquarium di Lucus Feroniae (Capena, Italy). See pp.40 & 41 for details from this depiction. (R. D'Amato)

Head of a gladiator, probably an *eques*, from the Casone Collevecchio (Italy). (Author's drawing)

prisoners of war, because they were familiar with the profession of arms. Many slaves were also obtained in the markets, largely supplied by pirates; Pompey's naval campaign of 67 BC put an end to such activity, however, and cut off this source of supply. Slaves also arrived via the Gauls, who bartered thousands of them for Italian goods, especially wine. Appian (*Bella Civilia* I.14.116) and Plutarch (*Crassus* VIII.3) tell us that a certain number were directly transferred to the owners of *ludi*. These *lanistae* (managers of gladiator schools) also recruited directly in prisons or agricultural estates, for which activities Cicero criticizes a friend (*Pro Sext.* LXIV.134). With or without their slaves' consent, some masters also sent slaves to barracks to learn the trade. If the slaves became champions, they hoped to win fame and fortune. Such masters may also have wanted to make these slaves their bodyguards, or reserve them for exhibitions in the inner circle.

The first voluntary engagements (*auctorationes*) took place a few years after the Spartacus revolt. It is difficult to estimate the percentage of volunteers (*auctorati*). If they are taken to represent one-third of the gladiators in the 1st century AD (according to our documentation), they were much less numerous in the 1st century BC. They came from all walks of life, from freed slaves to noblemen, but were still rare. The first known to us is a knight by the name of Furius Leptinus. Others imitated him, which led the Senate to legislate in 46 BC to prohibit such exhibitions staged by noblemen, which were infamous because they were public and paid.

The poorest looked to the *ludi* for a way to support themselves or their families. Indeed, the engagement bonus was not negligible, nor were the rewards for each victory, even for a son of a good family saddled with debts. Others sought to escape idleness, or hoped to become distinguished by the use of arms. There were undoubtedly among them many uprooted peasants, artisans and shopkeepers deprived of their work, for the numbers of unemployed in Rome were enormous. There were also men of questionable morals, and demobilized soldiers whose experience of arms naturally interested the *lanistae*.

Coerced slaves and convicts had no choice of career. Free men and volunteers had to apply before the tribune of the plebs, in Rome, or before

A **FUNERAL DUELS, CAMPANIA, 4TH CENTURY BC**
These three Lucanian warriors of the 4th century BC are representative of the men who clashed during the funeral games. They are the ancestors of the first gladiators of the *Samnites armatura*. They are inspired by frescoes discovered in several necropolises around the ancient city of Paestum in Campania.

(1) Lucanian warrior, c.320–315 BC
This figure, based upon a tomb painting in the necropolis of Andriuolo, is a wealthy man, capable of owning a horse and full equipment. His Italo-Chalcidian helmet is spectacular, with a bronze crest, wings and feathers. The artefact is in the Museo archeologico nazionale del Melfese "Massimo Pallottino" (Italy). His breastplate is a white *linothorax*, worn over a beige tunic. Typical of this region, he wears a large bronze belt, which is a symbol of virility; it remained an accessory for gladiators for centuries. The decorated shield comes from a fresco in the necropolis of Vannulo.

(2) Lucanian warrior, c.350 BC
This warrior is completely naked under his panoply, perhaps for a religious reason. Based on armour held at the Museo

archeologico nazionale di Paestum (Capaccio Paestum, Italy), his trilobed armour, typical of the peoples of Samnium, is made up of two similar plates (ventral and dorsal), held by wide bronze straps. With an original crest mount, the helmet also comes from Paestum. His conical shield is made of woven wicker, covered with leather. His weapons are javelins that are intended to be used like *banderillas*.

(3) Lucanian warrior, 375–350 BC
This man wears neither breastplate nor helmet, and is protected only by a pair of greaves and his shield, the latter a wooden *hoplon* (or *aspis*) covered with leather or metal. A bronze belt encircles his highly decorated tunic; the Romans laughed at these colourful tunics. Few frescoes show funeral battles with swords.

(4) Referee, c.365 BC
Funeral duels were conducted under the control of referees, like all athletic competitions. This depiction is based upon a fresco at Paestum. He too wears a bronze belt, along with his loosely draped garment. He wields a long flexible wand to enforce his decisions; it is the symbol of his function. In his other hand, he holds the crown that will be presented to the winner.

the provincial governor. These authorities could reject the applicants if they were deemed physically or psychologically unfit, but also sometimes on social grounds (especially if they were noble). Those who were accepted were then enlisted. In addition to recording the name and age of the volunteer, the contract also noted the duration of the engagement, for a defined time or number of fights. Finally, a salary was decided. Then the postulants took the oath, declaring that they accepted to sell themselves, as a slave was sold; this is the original meaning of the verb *auctorare*. Each one accepted being 'burned, chained, struck, killed' – (*flammis*) *uri, vinciri,* (*virgis*) *verberari, ferro necari* – which were all punishments reserved for slaves (Horace, *Satirae* II.7.58–59). From then on, the *lanista* had a right of life and death over them.

The different fights

The first slave battles were systematically fatal for the losers. In a way, they were human sacrifices in front of funeral pyres. This does not mean that the winner was released, however; instead, he was undoubtedly reserved for future fights, until he too died. This was the case until the Spartacus revolt (our sources are silent for the 3rd and 2nd centuries BC). For a long time, no doubt, the *lanistae* must have been reluctant to see their gladiators die, those whom they had trained, housed and fed for a time. To the *lanistae*, every death was money lost. Sponsors of *munera* also needed to monitor their spending, as putting on a show cost a fortune. Indeed, when a gladiator breathed his last on the sand, they had to pay the *lanista* a purchase price for the corpse; but when the gladiator returned to his *ludus* alive, only a rental price had to paid. This system made it possible to compensate the *lanistae* for the loss of earnings. Death was therefore costly for everyone, and at the end of our period, fighting without killing was the most common form. The outcome of the fighting therefore had to be stipulated in the contracts.

The system we know for the Principate, possibly instituted at the start of 'technical' gladiatorialism, and possibly revised by Augustus, defines three main types of fights. The first level offered simple technical exhibitions, with weapons that had been rendered harmless. The second level was called *ad digitum*, literally 'on the finger'. In this case, the weapons were real and lethal. A gladiator was forbidden from killing his opponent during combat,

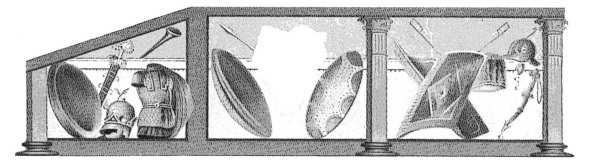

however; instead, he had to make him give up the fight, the defeated gladiator raising an index finger to signify his surrender. Only those gladiators who were deemed not to have had a good fight were killed. Death was, therefore, an exceptional sanction. The third and final degree was the combat *sine missione* (or '*apotomoï*' in the East), that is to say a combat which necessarily ended with the death of the vanquished. It is not clear whether referees officiated during this type of duel.

ABOVE & BELOW

A frieze of weapons and equipment from Pompeii (Italy) is depicted in these drawings, based on a watercolour by the artist Michele Mastracchio, dating from 1837. Mastracchio's watercolour is an invaluable resource that sheds light on some of the main *armaturae* in the middle of the 1st century BC. (Author's drawings)

THE *ARMATURAE*

Originally, the Campanians do not seem to have made any distinctions between fighters; the *armaturae* were probably an invention of the Etruscans. Still low in number at the end of the Republic, their number increased during the first half of the 1st century BC, notably during Augustus' reforms. This was a time when gladiatorialism was undergoing a new transformation, as a need for novelty demanded to be satisfied. We currently know of about 15 categories of gladiators, but not all of them were created from the start; and we are only interested in those known to exist during these first four centuries. These *armaturae* are easily identifiable by the particular equipment of their combatants, and the resultant fighting techniques.

During the Principate, the Romans made a distinction between *scutati* (gladiators equipped with large shields) and *parmati* (gladiators bearing small shields). The spectators had their preferences, often between 'big shields' (*scutati*) and 'small shields' (*parmati*), and sometimes they too fought in the stands like present-day football hooligans. Here, we discuss the *scutati* – the *Samnis, Gallus, essedarius, mirmillo* and *provocator* – first, before covering the *parmati*, namely the *Thraex, hoplomachus* and *eques*. Those gladiators who did not carry shields – the *retiarius, sagittarius* and *andabata* – are discussed last.

These two warriors are equipped with the *clipeus*, the great shield of the hoplites. This depiction is held at the Museo archeologico nazionale di Paestum. (G. Habasque)

The *Samnis*

The *Samnis* was the oldest gladiator, and yet he is the one about whom the least is known. His original appearance is well understood, thanks to the texts, an abundant iconography and many archaeological discoveries. On the other hand, this gladiator type's final aspect remains mysterious. In the 4th century BC, the Samnites and the Romans fought a series of bitter wars. Livy explains the origin of the *Samnites* as a gladiator type in a famous text that describes their defeat at the hands of the Romans and their Campanian allies in 310 BC, as well as their equipment:

> Here is the description of the shield: it was in its upper part wider to protect the chest and shoulders and tapered downwards so as not to interfere with movement. A breastplate covered the chest and only

B **'ETHNIC' GLADIATORS, 3RD–2ND CENTURIES BC**

A relief from Amiternum (see pp.19 & 44), held at the Museo nazionale d'Abruzzo (L'Aquila, Italy), undoubtedly shows a ritual fight between two *Galli*, equipped with special outfits, as the historian Polybius testifies (*Hist.* III.62.5). The winner will take the feather of his opponent, like a trophy. The typology of certain weapons indicates a Celtic origin, and a dating between the 3rd and 2nd centuries BC.

(1) *Gallus*, 3rd–2nd centuries BC
The man's head is bare, surrounded by a band in which a feather is stuck. He wears a short chain-mail shirt, an invention of the Celts, and a leather belt with an iron chain for hanging a Gallic sword, with a fabric belt placed over the top. A bronze greave – a borrowing from the Italic tradition – protects his left leg. His right hand is protected by a leather mitt.

(2) *Gallus* assistant
This young man is not Gallic. He only assists the *Gallus* in his duel, giving him spears and allowing him to continue the fight when the previous spear is broken or lost.

(3) *Gallus*, 2nd century BC
This *Gallus* is based upon a depiction on a stone urn (see p.18) kept at the Musée Calvet (Avignon, France). He is naked, to correspond to the stereotype of Greco-Roman literature. His flat shield is rectangular, but it could have another shape. The torque he wears was found in Fenouillet (France). His weapon is a sword, attached to the belt with a metal chain.

(4) *Thraex*, start of 2nd century BC
Captured in Thrace by the Romans, this prisoner of war is based on a depiction in the Sashova mogila tomb (Kazanluk, Bulgaria). His weapon is the long, almost straight scythe called a *romphaia*; it will shorten over time, to become the *sica*. His helmet is in the Phrygian style, characterized by the globular crest; the cheekpieces simulate a beard.

(5) 'Celto-German' gladiator, late 2nd–early 1st century BC
The Roman historian Sallust testifies to the existence of many Germans in the army of Spartacus. They are surely the descendants of the vanquished of the great migration of Cimbri and Teutons, augmented by other Celto-Germanic peoples. This figure is inspired by a bronze situla found in Pompeii. The torque is reproduced from an artefact from Tayac (France). The sword's round pommel suggests the use of a Roman sword in place of an 'ethnic' sword. At this time, the outfits gradually became less 'ethnic', and more codified. The decoration of the hexagonal shield is visible on the situla. It also shows two spears. We understand that the duel began with the spear and ended with the sword.

the left leg was protected. The soldiers wore a helmet topped with an egret to appear taller. [...] The Romans at least kept the weapons of the enemies to pay homage to the gods; but the Campanians, out of contempt and hatred of the Samnites, used them to arm the gladiators who performed at banquets and to whom the name of Samnites remained. (Livy, *Ab Ur. Con.* IX.40)

This is certainly an invention *a posteriori*, to explain the creation of this *armatura*. Indeed, the first 'gladiatorial' scenes illustrating the tombs of Campania date from the years 390–380 BC, that is to say 70–80 years earlier. Livy focuses on the shield, which he calls a *scutum*, a long shield of bentwood covered with leather; however, this shield is not visible on images from the 4th century BC. The numerous representations of this period show *clipei*, which were round and lenticular shields. It is therefore likely that Livy commits an anachronism, by giving the ancient Samnites the shield that equipped the *Samnites* in his time. This flared shield may have existed between these two periods, however, which would have led to its adoption by gladiators bearing the same designation.

The appearance of the *Samnis* can be supplemented by a few rare details gleaned from other authors. Varro (*De Lingua Latina* V.142) confirms the presence of long feathers (*pinnae*) on the helmet, and Cicero (*De Oratore* II.325) apparently gives the *Samnis* spears, but which are more likely javelins (*vibrant hastas*), which the *Samnis* uses before transitioning to his sword for close combat. The 4th-century BC frescoes show that the javelins were not necessarily thrown at the opponent, but could be thrust at him, like the *banderillas* of a toreador.

Despite these clues, it is very difficult to identify a *Samnis* in the iconography of the 1st century BC. A mural from Pompeii (Italy) – now lost, but reproduced in 1837 by Michele Mastracchio (see p.13) – may shed some light. We see in it the panoply of gladiators leaning on a balustrade. The typology of the weapons indicates a dating from the middle of the 1st century BC; it would therefore be one of the oldest and most valuable documents of 'technical' gladiatorism. One of these sets could be the

The ancestor of the *Samnis* gladiator often fought naked, at funeral competitions. This depiction is held at the Museo archeologico nazionale di Paestum. (R. D'Amato)

A pair of gladiators from the late 1st century BC or early 1st century AD, depicted in this find from Nesce (Italy), now held at the Colosseum (Rome, Italy). This depiction probably represents the ultimate version of the Samnite *armatura*. (G. Habasque)

weaponry of the *Samnis*, as we recognize apparently flared *scuta*. Behind emerge two straight metal rods, like spits, with square handles. Here we have, perhaps, the late version of the *banderillas*. The helmet is capped with a single feather at the top, and next to it is a sword. A bas-relief from Nesce (Italy) could show the ultimate stage of this *armatura*.

When and why did this old *armatura* disappear? Some said it had been transformed, or changed its name; for others, its disappearance was because Augustus no longer wanted to upset the Samnites, who had long since become Roman citizens. Indeed, a few documents (*CIL* 9.466 & AE 1988.27) prove the existence of the Samnites in the 1st century AD, and even during the reign of Nero (AD 54–68), but they were like the last of the dinosaurs. Rather, we can imagine that the declining Samnite *armatura* distributed some of its peculiarities to one or another of the new *armaturae* that were being created at the same time, in terms of equipment and combat techniques: the feathers, the pectoral, the practice of fighting with two weapons. Once these transfers were ratified, the survival of the Samnite *armatura* could no longer be justified; its eclipse was perhaps precipitated because it no longer presented any uniqueness, and therefore no interest.

Like all ethnic *armaturae*, the *Samnites* fought among themselves. Lucilius (*Satires* IV.9) says that the *Samnis* Eserninus was opposed to the best gladiator of his time, a certain Pacideianus, of whom Cicero also speaks, and who was in fact a *Samnis* himself.

The *Gallus*

The first mention of this gladiator is provided by Livy (*Ab Ur. Con.* XXXIX.42.11), for the year 184 BC, but there is no doubt that the *Gallus* had been in existence for a long time by this point. Since the 4th century BC, the Gauls had been fierce enemies of the Etruscans and then the Romans. They invaded Italy and occupied the north of the peninsula, even besieging Rome and its last defenders on the Capitol in 390 BC. Having Celtic prisoners of war fight was also a way to exorcise the fear these barbarians inspired in the Romans, and to show that they were not immortal.

Some images exist of Gallic gladiators in the 3rd and 2nd centuries BC. They are almost always shown naked, or half-naked, with a torque around the neck, and with shaggy hair to mark their barbaric character. They are helmetless and carry only a sword suspended from a belt, as well as a flat, oval, hexagonal or rectangular shield. The *Galli* therefore fought with their national armaments, like all 'ethnic' gladiators at that time. Their 'nudity', purportedly displaying their contempt for death, was a topic of Greco-Roman literature. In reality, however, only the nobles (and their guards) carried complete equipment; the bulk of the Gallic forces were lightly armed. We know from Polybius (*Historiai* III.62.5) the existence of ritual duels between Gallic chiefs, who donned special outfits for such occasions. We certainly have an image of it with a relief from Amiternum (held at the Museo nazionale d´Abruzzo; see pp.19 & 44) in which two warriors clash with heavy equipment. Assistants give them spears (or long javelins) to continue the fight. The shape of the hilt of their swords, the shield shape and the *umbo* (boss) suggest Celtic weaponry. The typology of the *umbo* allows the scene to be dated to the end of the 3rd century BC. The distinctive leggings shown, and the feather planted in a band on the forehead, strongly suggest that this is a depiction of gladiators.

In the 1st century BC, the sword used was now systematically the Roman *gladius*. The *Gallus* was devoid of body protection, except for his short armband and a very simple helmet with cheekpieces, and lacking a crest. We can see depictions of *Galli* on a relief at Venafro (Italy), on a very clear relief at the Museo Civico Archeologico di Bologna (italy), on a goblet attributed to Chrysippus (Lyon, France), and even on some oil lamps. The gladiator wears only a loincloth; his shield is flat and oval.

The *Galli* fought each other, but the motif of an oil lamp shows us a *Thraex* facing a *Gallus*. This suggests a phase of trial and error, in search of the optimal pairings. An inscription from Venosa (Italy), dated to the beginning of the 1st century AD, mentions *mirmillones* and *Galli*. This

Two naked *Galli* fight next to a funeral urn in this depiction displayed at the Musée Calvet (Avignon, France). (Author's drawing)

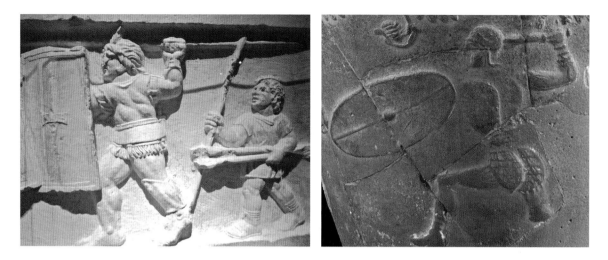

coexistence invalidates the hypothesis that the *mirmillo* was the descendant of the *Gallus*. In any case, mentions of *Galli* are rare. Although this category had its heyday for several centuries, it became a secondary *armatura* at the beginning of the Principate. It is possible that it evolved into another *armatura*, whose name it gradually took: that of the *essedarii*, at the turn of the Republic and the Principate. The *Galli* do not seem to have remained in existence by the 2nd century AD.

The *essedarius*

The *essedarius* was a warrior who fought on the platform of a chariot (Caesar, *BG* IV.24). This name comes from the word *essedum*, which designated a chariot among the Celts (Servius, after Virgil, *Ad Georg.* III.204). The origin of this *armatura* must therefore be sought among the Gallic peoples. Beyond this certainty, we do not know its genesis. The most widely held hypothesis is that the first *essedarii* were brought back from Britain by Caesar. In 55 and 54 BC, his legions crossed the Channel and fought against the chariots of the islanders. Caesar was greatly impressed, and left a long description of their use. The chronology of Cicero's correspondence, which first mentions this *armatura* in a letter (*Ad fam.* VII.10.2), suggests that its creation may have been earlier, however.

Other hypotheses can be put forward. For example, the Boii, a Gallic tribe, still deployed chariots on the battlefield in the 2nd century BC. Livy (XXXVI.38) relates that Scipio's army captured 247 chariots during the summer of 190 BC. These vehicles took part in the triumphal parade in Rome, three years later. They could then be presented in a big show to please the people.

Images of gladiators from before the Principate are very rare, so it is unsurprising that we do not see a lot of *essedarii*. As for the chariot, it was never represented, even during the Principate. The chariot was not a weapon of war for the Celts; rather, it was a means of transport for their chiefs, who dismounted to fight. During combat, drivers waited nearby, ready to evacuate them. Following their example, the new *essedarii* were to arrive in a chariot driven by a coachman. Caesar (*BG* IV.33) says the British warriors threw javelins from the tops of chariots. This is conceivable in war, but in gladiatorial combat these javelins could injure or kill the driver or the horses. We do know that the *essedarius* was armed with a spear, with which

Held at the British Museum (London, UK), this lead figurine depicts a provincial *essedarius* wielding his sword. (S. Lagrange)

he had to hit his opponent (another *essedarius*), no doubt when the chariots crossed. They then had to dismount from their chariots and fight on foot with swords.

> This is the way these chariots fight: first, they fly them all over the place by throwing missiles; the mere fear inspired by horses and the noise of the wheels usually throws disorder into the ranks; then, when they have penetrated between the squadrons, they jump from their chariots, so that, if the combatants are pressed for numbers, they can fall back on them conveniently. They thus combine in combat the mobility of the rider and the solidity of the infantryman, and the effect of their training and their daily exercise is such that they can stop their horses launched on a fast track, moderate them and make them turn quickly, run on the pole, stand firm on the yoke, and from there get into their chariot in an instant. (Caesar, *BG* IV.33)

With this reading, we understand why the Romans wanted to include these chariots in the gladiatorial games. Except in the circus, the performance areas were simply too small to allow the chariots to be manoeuvred. Moreover, once the real duel on foot had started, the chariot was of no use. This undoubtedly quickly lessened its interest in the eyes of the spectators, and perhaps the chariot was very quickly abandoned.

Another interesting peculiarity had to exist for the *essedarii* to survive as an *armatura* without their chariots, however. Their fighting technique was highly distinctive. The Gauls used long swords, which were wielded primarily by striking from above. Some even lacked a point. In contrast, the Romans preferred sword-edged fencing. This required more energy, and the punches were less effective. In addition, raising the arm to strike exposed the fighter's right flank. Images dating from the end of the Republic and the beginning of the Principate show swords lacking points in the hands of the *essedarii*. At that time, the weapon was no longer the Celtic long sword, but

Held at the Museo archeologico di Terni, this depiction of a confrontation between two *essedarii* dates from the end of the 1st century BC or the beginning of the 1st century AD. They appear to be bareheaded, but must be wearing wig-covered helmets. (N. Ledouble)

a shorter Roman sword, with its tip removed. These gladiators therefore had to give violent blows, only with the edge of the weapon, which was an unusual, almost barbaric technique in the eyes of the spectators.

It is logical that *Galli* replaced the first Celtic prisoners of war exhibited on chariots. Their 'ethnic' outfit was almost similar. But the greater originality exhibited by the *essedarii* was perhaps detrimental to the fortunes of the *Galli*, who quickly disappeared at the end of our period of study.

The fighting style exhibited by the *essedarii*, striking with the edge of the sword, exposed the head. It is therefore possible that a special 'face' helmet was designed for the *essedarii*, as suggested by a bas-relief from Dyrrhachium (now Durres, Albania). Ancient iconography more often shows *essedarii* wearing open helmets, like those of other gladiators. With the replacement of the long sword with the truncated sword, the shield also evolved, becoming curved and therefore more enveloping and protective, like those of Roman soldiers.

Detail of a fresco of the House of the Priest Amandus in Pompeii. Reproduced in a 1928 publication by the Accademia Nazionale dei Lincei, this is perhaps the first illustration of a *mirmillo*. (Author's drawing)

The *mirmillo*

In his *Philippicae*, dated 44 BC, Cicero is the first writer to testify to the existence of the *mirmillo*. This *armatura* therefore probably appeared a few years earlier, if not a few decades. This was a 'technical' *armatura* that no longer has any connection with a defeated enemy nation. Perhaps we have a first image in the House of the Priest Amandus in Pompeii, dated *c*.80–70 BC. Florus writes (II.8.12) that Spartacus was a *mirmillo*, but this is not certain.

Armed with a straight military sword, the *mirmillo* had a large semi-cylindrical shield, the *myrmillonicum scutum*. At first, its side edges were still convex. It was essentially a legionary's *scutum*, but with the ends cut off to make it lighter. The adoption of this form of shield by the gladiators predated

A defeated *mirmillo* observes the clash of two *provocatores*. Dating from the end of the 1st century BC, this bas-relief found in Rome is particularly detailed. Held at the Museo Nazionale Romano, Terme di Diocleziano (Rome, Italy). (G. Habasque)

its adoption by the military by several decades. The *mirmillo* also had a short pad on his left leg, as this part of the body was not protected by the large shield. His helmet was a Hellenistic-type model, common to several *armaturae*. A very late and ambiguous text (Festus, *De verb. signif.*: *retiarius*) suggested that the helmet was decorated with a representation of a fish, but this text has been misinterpreted. Some have tried to find a connection between the name *mirmillo* (or *myrmillo*, *murmillo* or even *mormillo*) and a fish, such as the moray eel (*muraena*), or the morme (*murmoros*), or even the *murex* snail, because of its bristled shells covered in spines. But no assumption is really satisfactory.

The *mirmillo*'s weaponry and fighting style brought him closer to the Roman legionary, and perhaps this new category was created to symbolize the soldier of Rome against his enemies. The type's known opponents were, to begin with, the *Thraex* (this was the most popular duel at the end of the Republic), then the *hoplomachus*, and later the *retiarius*. This last duel had only a short existence. Indeed, the angular helmet crest of the *mirmillo* snagged too easily in the net, which was a disadvantage.

A *mirmillo* adopts a combat position in this depiction, dating from the last third of the 1st century BC and held at the Museo del Sannio (Benevento, Italy). (N. Ledouble)

C

GLADIATORS, EARLY 1ST CENTURY BC

This representation is essentially based on a fresco in the House of the Priest Amandus in Pompeii. It illustrates a show in the amphitheatre, as evidenced by the presence of a musician. The fresco is damaged, however, and the *armaturae* are difficult to identify. The equipment became lighter and standardized in the 1st century BC.

(1) *Mirmillo*, c.80–70 BC

This man fights topless. His conical helmet looks like a Montefortino model; here it is devoid of metal cheekpieces, and it only has a simple leather chinstrap. His shield, known as the *myrmillonicum scutum*, is the great *scutum* of the legionary, but the ends have been truncated to make it lighter. His sword is the long *gladius Hispaniensis* used by the Roman Army.

(2) *Eques*, c.80–70 BC

On the same fresco is visible a duel of *equites*, possibly commemorating the death of Spartacus, as the name 'Spartaks' is written above the wounded rider. The horse has a Gallic saddle of the style recently adopted by the Roman Army. It is made of leather with four horns, to stabilize the rider without stirrups. The gladiator's panoply is difficult to identify. He wears a linen breastplate, extended by *pteryges*, inspired by contemporary sculptures from the temple of Juno Sospita in Lanuvium (modern-day Lanuvio, Italy). He carries a sword on his left hip, but first fights with a spear. His helmet is an Attico-Boeotian model, characterized by its large wavy brim; the sheet-metal crest simulates a horsehair crest. Like all *equites* of the 1st century BC, he wears long hair. His shield is a *parma equestris* formed from cowhide; its large diameter will be reduced under Augustus. Its white colour is visible on a frieze from Pompeii. The *eques* wears shoes, unlike other gladiators.

(3) *Essedarius*, c.100 BC

This reconstruction is hypothetical, as there is no image of an *essedarius* on a chariot; this depiction is based on the archaeological record. As the gladiator cannot both fight and drive the chariot, it is driven by a coachman. After a phase fighting with javelins or the spear, the *essedarius* continues the combat on foot. The sword used by this prisoner of war has a rounded end, as it is intended to strike with the edges only. This particular form of fencing will justify the survival of this *armatura*, but the chariot will be definitively abandoned.

The *provocator*

Another possible candidate for the inauguration of 'technical' gladiatorialism is the *provocator*. Like the *mirmillo*, this type was not named after a defeated enemy of Rome. Its name comes from its fighting technique. *Provocare* in fact means 'the one who provokes' (in a duel). This name suggests an energetic technique, where the gladiator came into contact, and immediately refused it, in order to feign, provoke his opponent and prompt him to make a mistake. One can easily imagine a kind of dance, during which the shields slice the air.

We do not know the reasons that led to the creation of the *provocator*. From the outset, he seems to have fought only colleagues of the same *armatura*. Cicero is the first to evoke this gladiator, in a plea dated 56 BC (before the first mention of the *mirmillo*, but this does not certify its anteriority): 'But, as we have seen, not to choose champions in the markets, but to buy in the *ergastula* the scraps of the vilest slaves to decorate them with the name of gladiators, and to randomly turn them into *Samnites* or *provocatores*: should we not fear the consequences of such a culpable license and such contempt for the law?' (Cicero, *Pro Sext.* LXIV.134). This excerpt from Cicero contradicts a widely accepted theory today, which posits that the *armatura* of *provocatores* replaced that of *Samnites*, no doubt on the basis that *provocatores* sported a pectoral, as the Samnite warriors once wore. But the pectoral had always been very common in Italy. On the contrary, this text clearly shows that the two *armaturae* coexisted, for several decades, until the extinction of the *Samnites*.

Dating from the end of the 1st century BC, this stele from Dyrrachium (Albania) shows a left-handed *provocator*. Now held at the Narodni muzej (Belgrade, Serbia). (Author's drawing)

Traces of the *provocator* were rare at the end of the Republic. The type does not appear on the Fiano Romano relief (*c.*10 BC). Even in depictions from Pompeii, he remains very rare. Therefore, some historians believe that this *armatura* was a special category for trainee gladiators: the first level of a pseudo-gladiator curriculum. The sources very easily contradict this hypothesis, however.

The *provocator*'s shield (*parma*) had convex edges. It was smaller, and therefore lighter, than the great *scutum* of the *mirmillo* or the *essedarius*. This saving in weight allowed it to be better used as an offensive weapon, by slicing at the opponent with it. Hoplomachy was more violent, and therefore more spectacular for the audience, but it required the wearing of a pectoral attached at the back by straps, to protect against these blows. This breastplate was the distinguishing mark of the *provocator*. On the Tiber relief, held at the Museo Nazionale Romano (Italy), the helmet worn by the *provocator* is different from the Hellenistic model common to many *armaturae*. It mixed certain characteristics with those of a new military helmet that would be widely developed under the Principate, the Weisenau type, distinguished by a low, very accentuated neck protector, and a cutout around each ear.

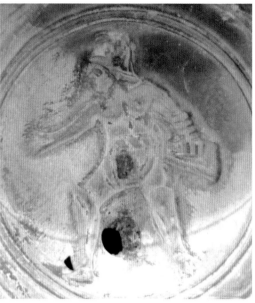

The *Thraex*

Its name indicates that this *armatura* was created with prisoners captured from the Thracians, inhabitants of a region whose ancient borders encompassed parts of present-day Bulgaria, Greece and Turkey. Pliny the Elder (*Hist. Nat.* IV.18) refers to the Thracians as one of the most powerful peoples in Europe at that time. Mercenary activity was very widespread there, and the states of Greece and Asia had always recruited peltasts (light infantry, mainly velites).

Once again, the first evocations of this *armatura* are provided by Cicero (*Philippicae* VI.5 & VII.6), around the middle of the 1st century BC. Some have therefore looked for an event close to this time to explain its creation. They linked its appearance with Sulla's military operations against Mithridates VI Eupator, ruler of Pontus (r. 120–63 BC), whose army included many soldiers from Thrace, during the First Mithridatic War (89–85 BC) (Appian, *Bella Mithridatica* VII.45). In fact, many other earlier conflicts can explain the presence of Thracian captives in Italian *ludi*. Roman historians recount in detail the recurring clashes between the Romans and the Thracians: in 187 BC (Livy, *Ab Ur. Con.* XXXVIII.40–41 & 49); in 171 BC; in 168 BC when King Perseus of Macedon (r. 179–168 BC) was defeated by the Romans at Pydna (Livy, *Ab Ur. Con.* XLII.12 & XLII.51); in 144 BC; in 93 BC (Orosius, *Historiae Adversum Paganos* I.5), etc. The name and composition made it an *armatura* from the era of 'ethnic' gladiatorialism, so its origins can therefore undoubtedly be dated prior to the 1st century BC. It is hard to imagine that only *Samnites* and *Galli* fuelled the gladiator games for three centuries, without the appearance of new types and fighting techniques.

The array of ancient Thracian warriors is clearly visible on ancient ceramics, and many artefacts have been found. The *Thraex armatura* differs, however, from that of the *Thraeces* we know at the end of our period. Unfortunately, we lack information to understand the reasons for the evolution of this *armatura*.

Bare-legged at first, the *Thraex* adopted leg coverings made up of bands (*fasciae*) for both legs, to supplement the limited protection afforded by his small, square, curved shield. His sword had a curved blade, as if to bypass

ABOVE LEFT
A *Thraex* depicted on an oil lamp. The shape of his sword is characteristic of the 1st century BC. The oil lamp is held at the Römisch-Germanisches Museum. (B. Kueppers)

ABOVE RIGHT
This left-handed *Thraex* has been defeated; the position of his right hand indicates that he will not be pardoned. This depiction is held at the Museo Civico Archeologico di Bologna. (N. Ledouble)

obstacles and inflict injuries from unusual angles. This type of sword was based upon those in use among Thracian warriors, but in longer formats. Another iconic element of the *Thraex*'s outfit was his helmet. Initially without a visor, such helmets often took the shape of Phrygian caps and helmets; the characteristic protuberance at the front was transformed into a crest on which was added a *protome* (a representation of the upper part) of a griffin, a mythological animal considered to be a psychopomp, a guardian of the world of the dead. This griffin was not yet synonymous with this *armatura* – it does not appear on a Chrysippus goblet – but it became so at the beginning of the 1st century AD.

Like all 'ethnic' gladiators, the *Thraex*'s first duels took place within the same *armatura*, which is confirmed by some ceramics from La Graufesenque

This shard from a Chrysippus goblet depicts a *Thraex*, c.20 BC. The goblet is held at the Musée Lugdunum. (Photo J.M. Degueule, Ch. Thioc / Lugdunum. Lyon, Musée Lugdunum)

5   cm

(a pottery production site in Millau, France) and a few surviving oil lamps. The recent discovery of a new fragment of the Fiano Romano relief shows this very clearly. At the end of the Republic, the *Thraex* was more systematically opposed to the *mirmillo*, the perfect balance provided by their different equipment unleashing the passions of spectators. The *Thraex* also fought against the *hoplomachus*, a pairing visible especially on the Fiano Romano relief and the work of Chrysippus.

The *hoplomachus*

The *hoplomachus* seems to have appeared later than the *Thraex*, perhaps only at the beginning of the Principate, because even Cicero does not mention that *armatura* (although he reveals to us for the first time the existence of the *essedarius*, the *provocator*, the *mirmillo* and the *Thraex*). But the absence of proof is not proof. The first iconographic evidence for the type is perhaps a bas-relief from the Museo Stefano Bardini (Florence, Italy). The shape and size of the defensive weapons suggest that the dating could be around the middle of the 1st century BC. We find the *hoplomachus* on one of the famous goblets from the Lyon workshop, in the last third of the 1st century BC. The type also appears several times on the Fiano Romano relief. On the other hand, the first inscription which evokes this gladiator comes from Venosa, and it dates only from the end of the reign of Augustus (*CIL* 9.4466).

The programmes recovered at Pompeii tell us about the *hoplomachus*' opposition to the *Thraex*. The letter 'O' indicates the *hoplomachus* (or *oplomachus*), while the letter 'T' refers to the *Thraex*. Armed with this information, it is easy to spot this duel on a large number of surviving images.

The term *hoplomachus* means 'heavily armed', and that is why, in the past, recreations of the type have been equipped with all possible, sometimes fanciful, arms and armour, including the large and heavy *scutum*. The term *hoplomachus* has the same origin as the term *hoplite*, the Greek heavy infantryman, or *hoplon*, his lenticular shield of wood and bronze, which is also called an *aspis*, and which the Romans called the *clipeus*. Thus, the equipment of the hoplite and the *hoplomachus* are very close. We can then ask ourselves the question as to the origin of this new gladiator: could the *hoplomachus* be of Greek or Macedonian origin? In the 2nd century BC, Roman forces fought the phalanxes of Perseus at the battle of Pydna, in

This terracotta statuette, originally enhanced with colour, depicts either a *Thraex* or – more likely – a left-handed *hoplomachus*. Held at the Museo archeologico nazionale di Taranto (Italy). (R. D'Amato)

168 BC, and conquered Greece. Sulla also intervened in Greece and besieged Athens in 87–86 BC. In his study of gladiatorialism in the Eastern Roman Empire, Louis Robert did not make reference to the *hoplomachus* at first, but later considered the type to be extremely rare (1940: 130). It is a fact that this *armatura* never found favour with the Greeks, although we often find it in the West. It is understandable that the Greeks were reluctant to present a gladiator who would ostensibly remind them of their submission to Rome. Conversely, this is perhaps what excited the imagination of the Romans: the *hoplomachus–mirmillo* duel (the latter type being able to be compared to the Roman soldier) would then evoke the historical dispute between Greeks and Romans.

The Greek hypothesis is not the only one, however. Although the Roman Army abandoned the round metal shield used in phalanx combat, instead adopting in the 4th century BC the large, curved shield – more suitable for the new Roman manipular tactics – in the armed forces of many other Italian cities the round shield remained in use. Numerous surviving Etruscan urns and funerary *stelae* bear witness to this, down to the 1st century BC. Could the *hoplomachus* represent Italian rivals to Rome? This hypothesis is conceivable, because the submission and loyalty of some Italians to Rome remained uncertain for a long time, as shown by the changes of alliances during the war against Hannibal in the 2nd century BC, or the Social War at the beginning of the 1st century BC. It is difficult to say whether this *armatura* was originally formed from Greek or Italian prisoners, which would refer us in both cases to 'ethnic' gladiatorialism, although the name *hoplomachus* rather suggests a 'technical' *armatura*.

The *hoplomachus* fought first with the spear. Should he lose his spear during the duel, the gladiator also had a sword, held in the same hand

---

D THE FIRST 'TECHNICAL' GLADIATORS, MID-1ST CENTURY BC

After the revolt of Spartacus, gladiatorialism was reformed to ensure its survival. The barracks were now also open to volunteers, and new *armaturae* appeared to increase the variety of combat.

(1) Hoplomachus, c.50 BC

This representation is based on a bas-relief in the Museo Stefano Bardini (Florence, Italy), which probably dates from the middle of the 1st century BC. The *hoplomachus* fights like a hoplite, with a lenticular shield and a spear. If he loses his long weapon, then he uses a sword. At that time, it was the *gladius Hispaniensis* used by the Roman Army. The three-lobed pommel is characteristic of this period. The diameter of the shield is still large. Its decoration is copied from a frieze of painted weapons from Pompeii. The gladiator wears a style of tunic known as the *exomis*, which reveals one shoulder. His Attico-Boeotian helmet is based upon an original held in the Museum für Kunst und Gewerbe Hamburg (Germany). His Greek-style greaves encompass the entire leg, and close behind the calf; leather gaiters prevent them from slipping down. On his right arm he wears an armband made of leather straps on a sheepskin sleeve.

(2) Sagittarius, c.50 BC

In the same bas-relief held at the Museo Stefano Bardini, two archers fight one another. Widely used in the Balkans, this man's conical helmet is a Hellenistic model surmounted by a moulded point. His loincloth is made of fur; it is worn with a bronze belt. His left arm is protected by a leather armband. The bow is a small model, with a double curvature. The number of hand-held arrows appears to be limited to three. The archer uses a thumb ring to tighten the string.

(3) Samnis, c.50 BC

This *Samnis* is reproduced from a frieze of weapons from Pompeii (see p.13), and an anachronistic description by Livy. He wears a leather doublet, reinforced by a square bronze pectoral. Livy confirms its use; he calls it *spongia pectori tegumentum* – literally 'the sponge that covers the chest' – because it 'absorbs' the blows of the opponent. His helmet is a Hellenistic model, with a feather on top. His shield is wider at the top, to cover his upper body, and narrower at the bottom, so as not to interfere with his legs. Initially, he fights with metal *banderillas*, using his sword subsequently.

(4) Thraex, c.50 BC

This *Thraex* is inspired by the bas-relief held at the Museo Stefano Bardini, and the frieze of arms of Pompeii. On the latter, we see a red Phrygian cap in sheepskin, the bottom of which is rolled up. His shield is rectangular in shape, medium in size, with classic decoration. He also wears small leather gaiters to better support the metal greaves. His weapon is an evolution of the *romphaia*, but its size has shortened to the length of a sword, and its curvature has reversed. Its blade has a central groove, and a protruding lug on one side.

that gripped the shield. He was not necessarily at an advantage, however, because he was handicapped by the way he held his shield. This rebalanced the opposition, as opponents of the *hoplomachus* had only one offensive weapon. In older images, the spear is held by its end, like the *banderilla* of the first combatants depicted on the tombs of Campania and Lucania. Should this be seen as a legacy of the *Samnites*? The *hoplomachus* also wore an armband, leggings identical to those of the *Thraeces*, and a helmet very similar to that of the *mirmillones*.

The *eques*

We do not know when and why this *armatura* was actually created. The first mention of the *eques* is communicated to us once again by Cicero (*Pro Sext.* LIX), which dates the type's appearance to at least the first half of the 1st century BC. According to Isidore of Seville (*Origines* XVIII.53), gladiatorial shows began with the confrontation of two horsemen who entered the arena through opposing doors, preceded by military ensigns whose presence indicated a desire to replay a historical scene.

The first known image of a duel of *equites* is on a fresco in the House of the Priest Amandus; this scene could commemorate the defeat of Spartacus, as the name 'Spartaks' is written above the horseman who has fled. It is important to remember, however, that this name was very common in Thrace, and the scene may represent another fighter altogether. Even so, one can easily imagine that fights between horsemen were organized very early on.

On this fresco, the panoply is not fully visible. On the other hand, for the end of our period, we see that the *equites* systematically wore a scaled breastplate, the origin of which was rather oriental. While literary or epigraphic references to the *armatura* are rare, representations are not uncommon. The most beautiful and precise is a bas-relief (see p.47) from the Glyptothek (Munich, Germany). With the inclusion of the breastplate,

Detail of the *equites* on the fresco of the House of the Priest Amandus. It illustrates, or perhaps commemorates, the defeat of Spartacus. (R. D'Amato)

the panoply is more military. The helmet is a classic Attico-Boeotian model. The sword wielded by the *eques* was long, so it could be wielded on horseback, and he also carried a spear to start the fight; however, a Principate-era oil lamp shows us a horseman armed with several javelins. The shield was the cowhide *parma equestris*, formerly in use by the Roman cavalry before the time of Polybius, but which endured as a symbol of their rank in the knightly class. Its use by gladiators does not indicate that such fighters were recruited from the equestrian order.

Held at the Antiquario Comunale, Isernia (Italy), this depiction of an *eques* features an Attico-Boeotian helmet and a *parma equestris*. (N. Ledouble)

Training *equites* was not feasible for all *ludi*, as such training required suitable structures for the reception and care of horses. Isidore of Seville tells us (*Orig.* XVIII.53) that the *equites* rode white horses. It is difficult to say whether this author gives an anecdotal description, and a somewhat belated one, or if he describes a tradition of *armatura*. The wall painting in the House of the Priest Amandus shows one white and one brown horse. The horses used by the Roman cavalry are known to us through several archaeological finds of skeletons and harness. They were small and sturdy with a stocky frame, measuring about 150cm at the withers.

Ancient iconography shows almost nothing but duels on foot. We do not know of any images of an *eques* on horseback fighting against an *eques* on foot. Are we to understand that, once one of the riders was unseated, the other was forced to dismount in order to continue the fight? This would deprive him of the advantage conferred by the superiority of his weapons, and penalize him unfairly. Rather, it can be assumed that horse fighting was time-limited, lest it drag on if one of the horses tried to avoid the confrontation. Indeed, if the duel of two infantrymen only lasted a few minutes at most – because of the exhaustion which very quickly affected both of the protagonists – it was different for the *equites*, neither of whom had any physical limitations other than those of their mounts. The dynamics of the show could be affected, however, and audiences might have tired of a never-ending fight. At the end of a set time, therefore, or once a spear was dropped or broken, or the javelins were all thrown, the referee might have forced the riders to dismount, to continue the fight on foot, and so shortened the duel. This is perhaps the most logical explanation.

The *retiarius*

The *retiarius* fought with a net (*rete*, hence the *armatura*'s name) and a trident. He was one of the best-known gladiators, and yet he was one of the last to be invented. This *armatura* seems to have been unknown under the Republic. The first figurative evidence of its existence appears on a goblet from the Atelier de la Muette (Lyon, France), fashioned by the potter Chrysippus *c.*15 BC. It is therefore reasonable to assume that the *armatura* of the *retiarii* was created only at the beginning of the Principate. Valerius Maximus, a contemporary of Augustus and Tiberius, informs us (*Fact.* I.8) that the adversary of the *retiarius* was the *mirmillo*.

It is difficult to know what motivated this original creation. There is nothing to link the new type with any weapon or military combat technique, as is the case with most other gladiator categories. Ancient literature twice mentions such a fight, however, which may have inspired the inventors of this *armatura*. According to Diodorus of Sicily (*Bibliotheca Historica* XVII.43.7–10), during the siege of Tyre conducted by the armies of Alexander the Great in 332 BC, the Tyrian defenders used long iron tridents to wound the besiegers; they also had some sort of net to envelop their opponents, and to draw them towards them or knock them down from the towers. They finally threw real nets on the drawbridges to thwart enemy assaults. Also, Strabo (a contemporary of Augustus) tells the story of Phrynon, leader of an Athenian army besieging the city of Sigeum in 606 BC, who perished in a duel against Pittacus of Mitylene. Clad as a fisherman, Pittacus 'entwined [Phrynon] in the mesh of his net, pierced him with his trident, and finished him with a stab' (*Geographica*, XIII.1.39).

Some have said that the *retiarius* was perhaps a foreshadowing of Neptune, the Roman god of the seas, and that the type was related to the celebration of Octavian's naval victory at Actium (31 BC), which brought him the imperial throne. This explanation is plausible, because the first performance of this new type of gladiator followed shortly after this major event. Isidore of Seville (*Orig.* XVIII.55) compares the *retiarius* to the sea god. Perhaps this new gladiator would have appeared in a show given in Lyon, capital of Gaul, to mark the visit of Augustus or Agrippa; the type would then have been imported to Italy, and would have evolved – but the gladiators reproduced on Chrysippus' ceramics are perhaps *Julianii*: that is to say, imperial gladiators, who came in the entourage of the emperor or his son-in-law, Marcus Vipsanius Agrippa.

Iconographic representations of the *retiarii* remained very rare at the beginning of the Principate. At that time it was still an *armatura* in search of the ideal opponent; and this meant that the *retiarii* fought among themselves, as suggested by the Scaurus monument in Pompeii. The Fiano Romano relief does not show the type, like that of the monument of Lusius Storax (Chieti, Italy), c.AD 15–20. In Pompeii, the first image is 70 years later than that of Chrysippus. In addition, the importance of the *retiarii* appears to be lower than that of other types, prompting the formulation of other hypotheses; one of their roles may have been to finish off death-row inmates during performances.

The *retiarius* is known today for the light weight of his equipment, which conferred speed and agility, but his first depiction, on the goblet of Chrysippus, features a helmet, chain mail and greaves. This early depiction represents a period of trial and error; the *retiarii* appear to have got rid of all this paraphernalia quickly. The *retiarius* wore a loincloth secured by a wide belt, an armband on the left arm (all the other gladiators wore an armband on the right arm, the one holding the weapon) and a shoulder plate to protect him from blows from his opponent. His offensive armament included a net to catch his adversary, a trident to keep him at bay and injure him and a dagger, usually held in the left hand. This last weapon was used in close combat, to deliver the fatal blow. The rare early images of this gladiator suggest that like the *eques*, and perhaps the *Samnis*, the *retiarius* retained his tunic by giving up his armour.

The *sagittarius*

The *sagittarius* fought an opponent from the same *armatura*. The type was known at the beginning of the Principate, because it is mentioned on the list of Venosa (*CIL* 9.465–66), but its existence must have been older, because we have two pieces of evidence that represent it, both dating from the 1st century BC.

Two *sagittarii*, presumably carrying no more than three or four arrows each, clash in this mid-1st century BC depiction held at the Museo Stefano Bardini. (N. Ledouble)

Details of *sagittarii* on the remains of a goblet from the potter Chrysippus. The goblet is held at the Musée Lugdunum. (Author's drawing)

The older of these is a bas-relief (see p.33) from the Museo Stefano Bardini, probably dating from the middle of the 1st century BC. Both archers depicted have only three or four arrows each, gripped in the same hand that is holding the bow; no quiver is visible. Carrying such minimal amounts of ammunition, these gladiators would have had no margin for error; they had to take risks to get as close as possible to their opponent, so as not to miss him. The danger was also great, however, so precision and speed were essential qualities of this *armatura*. One can imagine that the *sagittarius* was also forced to feint, and to exhibit great flexibility to dodge his adversary's arrows. In this depiction, the positions of the two men are very suggestive; one has fallen to his knees, injured in the leg by an arrow he is trying to extract. These *sagittarii* wear conical

helmets, like those worn by the archers of the Eastern cohorts of the Roman Army, which suggests a possible geographical origin for these gladiators or their *armatura*. They seem to be fighting shirtless. Beneath a wide belt each wears a crumpled-looking loincloth, which may possibly represent fur, perhaps to symbolize the barbarians they are meant to embody.

The second image is modelled on a goblet by the potter Chrysippus (see p.34), dating from the last quarter of the 1st century BC. On the right, an archer adopts a dynamic stance, ready to shoot his opponent, hit by two projectiles in the thorax (or in the arm that holds the bow), and another in one leg. Before he was hit, the injured archer had notched two arrows on his bowstring; this technique was unusual, but might have paid off in close combat. The round helmet worn in this depiction is another model: we see above it long, flowing hair, and for the victor, a curious appendage on the forehead, which must be a feather.

The arrows used in these combats would not have resembled those used in war, which were made to tear flesh. Rather, we can imagine that 'clean' arrows were used instead, these being capable of being extracted without causing too much damage, allowing the injured person to heal and conduct further duels. Vegetius (*De re militari* I.15) gives interesting details on the training of archers.

The *andabata*

The *andabata* is first mentioned by Cicero (*Ad fam.* VII.10.2), and Varro even gave this name to one of his satires. The *andabata* was to fascinate less with his technique, than to amuse the people with his involuntary antics. He was indeed fighting blind. The word *andabata* is of Gallic origin: it is made up of *ande*, meaning 'from below' (from the underworld, darkness ... hence the blindness), and *battuo*, which can be translated as 'beat'.

It is questionable, however, whether the *andabatae* were really gladiators, or simply condemned men whose lives were deemed to be worthless, offered to the public in cruel entertainment. Indeed, it is doubtful that men who had trained hard in the use of arms, and whose lives were precious to their *lanista* (because they were profitable), would have risked serious injury or death in grotesque exhibitions, the outcome of which was largely left to chance. Rather, the involvement of the *andabatae* evokes the *meridiani*, the bloody midday interludes in which convicts would die. Did such fighters really need to be trained in *ludi*? In 54 BC, in a letter to an officer of Caesar stationed in northern Gaul, Cicero (*Ad fam.* VII.10.2) gave the impression that the *andabatae* represented the worst of gladiatorialism. Fortunately, Chrysippus' workshop has left us with the only known depiction of the performance of a duel between *andabatae*, which provides us with precious details.

The *andabatae* were no longer discussed during the Principate, but it is plausible that they continued to exist under the name of *trinci* (or *trinqui*), mentioned in a text discovered in 1906 in Sardis (*CIL* 3.7106), which summarizes a more complete document called the Italica table. Dating from the 2nd century AD, this was a *senatus consultum* (a resolution or decree containing the advice of the Senate to the magistrates) drawn up under the emperor Marcus Aurelius (r. AD 161–80) that was intended to reduce the expense of gladiatorial shows. Corrected by French historian André Piganiol (1923: 62–71), the word *trinci* appears three times. According to the Italica table, the *trinci* were convicts whom the Gauls included in religious ceremonies, to be executed. After the Roman conquest of Gaul, the tradition

continued thanks to gladiatorial shows, which were a new way of carrying out this human sacrifice. The cities of Gaul bought them directly from the *lanistae* or from the procurator, from among the condemned (*damnati*). These men were not gladiators. This word is not used by the author of the entry, who refers instead to 'fencers' (*genus digladiantium*). The Italica table inscription specifies that they were not to be purchased for more than 2,000 sesterces (at the time of Marcus Aurelius) in the first case, and a little more than six gold coins in the second, 'on condition that they have taken an oath'. The price is not negligible; it seems to have been deliberately defined to deter and limit this type of execution, apparently frowned upon by the Romans, but maintained to satisfy the demand of the Gauls, and thus maintain concord. Indeed, the author of the Sardis text strongly disapproves of the games in which *trinci* appeared. The oath was supposed to be that of the condemned, according to the historian, which may be surprising since the condemned was not supposed to have had a say in the application of his punishment.

The present author believes that the *trinci* were the ancient *andabatae*, whose name etymology strongly suggests a funerary, and therefore religious, origin. We also know the ancient custom of singular combat among the Celts, and that of human sacrifices: elements that can be combined to explain the existence of the *andabatae*. These men therefore have their eyes 'opened' to 'prepare' them for their ultimate exhibition. This mutilation can be seen as 'immoral' from the Roman point of view. We can therefore understand why the authorities demanded that the convicts take an oath, which amounted to their offering to volunteer for this cruel fight. Indeed, being condemned to death, they would normally have had no chance of escaping their punishment: presumably a condemnation to beasts (*ad bestias*). They therefore had an alternative if they agreed to participate in this ancient ritual duel, agreeing to lose their sight, and risk serious injury. This arrangement can only have been feasible if the winner gained his life, and perhaps his freedom, but henceforth remained permanently blind.

This drawing depicting *andabatae* is copied from a Chrysippus goblet. The scene dates from *c*.20 BC, at a time when full-face gladiator helmets did not yet exist, and the eye openings could have been blocked. Here they wear open helmets, the cheekpieces of which are clearly visible. This would have meant that these fighters were truly blind. Logically, a man blind from birth would never have been educated in the art of combat. We must therefore strongly consider the possibility that these men had their eyes gouged out intentionally, with the intention of being involved in this exhibition, which therefore meant they were condemned men rather than gladiators. To find their bearings, each held a bell in his left hand, which also testified to their blindness, and designated them as an *andabata*. The *andabata* was armed with a sword; a shield was not considered necessary. He advanced cautiously, moving his sword in the air until it met an 'obstacle'. (Drawing by D. Bouet)

GLADIATOR GEAR

Over the first four centuries, the clothing and equipment of gladiators evolved logically; but if they were at first representative of the peoples who constituted the first *armaturae*, they definitely lost their 'ethnic' character in the 1st century BC, and gradually became standardized. Here we deal with gladiator clothing first, followed by body armour, helmets, shields and weapons.

Clothing

Modern observers are used to seeing gladiators with bare chests. This was not always true, or systematic, especially in the early days. *Samnites*, who clashed in funeral games, mostly wore **tunics** (*tunicae*). Such garments were not specifically military, as they were also worn for peaceful activities. They were generally very colourful, and were decorated with geometric patterns. The Roman audiences made fun of these brightly patterned clothes of which the frescoes of Paestum provide us with many examples. These tunics were made of wool, or of linen for the finest; they were short, and did not cover the thighs.

Some documents, however, show warriors naked, or half-naked, even if they wear a breastplate. Before gladiatorialism was codified, there were no rules of dress, so these early 'gladiators' used what they had. Rather, total nudity is a Greek athletic tradition of which the Romans disapproved; their modesty required the wearing of a minimum of clothing. Greco-Roman literature also often evokes the nudity of Gallic warriors. This was a cliché, but it is possible that the *lanistae* removed the clothes of their *Galli* to correspond to this stereotype of the naked Celt. The Gallic chiefs must have had more elaborate clothing, as the Amiternum relief suggests.

In the 1st century BC, the aspect of the gladiators was better known. By this time, most gladiators did not wear tunics. Gladiatorialism was now 'show business', and it had become important to take care of the setting and the costumes. Spectators wanted to see athletes in full swing. Gladiators who continued to wear armour continued to wear a tunic underneath it, however. This was true for the *equites*, the proto-*retiarii* and arguably also the *Samnites*. A bas-relief from Nesce shows two gladiators confronting each other under the gaze of a referee. Their panoply is original, due to their shield being in the shape of a *pelte* and their swords being straight; these details do not allow them to be easily attached to an identified *armatura*. Both fighters may be *Samnites*, in their ultimate evolution, during the reign of Augustus. They are dressed in tunics, which suggests that they were wearing breastplates before their equipment was lightened by the new imperial regulations. This hypothesis may be confirmed by the Pompeii fresco redrawn by Michele Mastracchio in 1837. Like the *Samnis*, the *eques* kept his tunic, after abandoning his breastplate. By this time, the tunic was a little looser, square in shape, and it could be decorated with vertical braid (*clavi*), either woven or added.

A special category of combatants could also wear a light, diaphanous tunic like that worn by courtesans. Because of this sartorial distinction, such gladiators were called *tunicati*. These men received little regard, and were kept apart in the *ludus*, to avoid promiscuity with other residents. This tunic was sometimes worn over one shoulder, to free an arm, and to facilitate fencing.

Campanian frescoes dating from the 4th century BC rarely show **loincloths**. We mostly see men in tunics, or naked. A few Etruscan images, from the 3rd or 2nd centuries BC, show gladiators shirtless, with some sort of 'skirt'; perhaps it is a tunic whose shoulder straps have been unhooked. The loincloth appears on bas-reliefs from the 1st century BC. At the end of the Republic, and at the very beginning of the Principate, this loincloth was made from a large piece of fabric that covered the posterior and formed a very pleated rounded shape at the front. A bronze belt kept the loincloth on the hips, thus freeing the wearer's leg movements. In Italian images from the latter half of the 1st century BC, below the waistband, a long strip of pleated fabric like a scarf emerges, which usually reaches down to the knees. It sometimes forms a visible 'lump' above the waistband. It is sometimes fringed, or even weighted with a ball on several gladiators (*Thraeces* and *hoplomachi* only) on the Fiano Romano monument. We cannot explain this last singularity, which is not systematic. Is this the distinctive mark of a *ludus*? The band of fabric disappears towards the change of eras. The relief from the Collezione Torlonia (Palazzo Orsini, Rome, Italy; see p.7), which probably represents the *venatio* given in 11 BC for the inauguration of the Theatre of Marcellus, shows gladiators who lack it. One can reasonably conclude that fashion had changed by this time. The abandonment or adoption of a piece of equipment never happens on a fixed date, however; it could take years to formalize, allowing different fashions to coexist. Later frescoes show that the loincloths were predominantly white. Other colours are seen but more rarely.

Alongside Italian fashion, it should be noted that there were indigenous versions of the loincloth (*subligar, subligaculum*). The ceramics of Lyon indeed show checked fabrics, typically Gallic, which even have fringes. On these artefacts, the fabric scarf on the front is absent. Undoubtedly earlier, a relief in the Museo Stefano Bardini shows two *sagittarii* dressed in loincloths that appear crumpled, or which were perhaps made of fur. This detail is also visible on the figurine of an *essedarius* held at the British Museum (see p.20).

The **belt** (*balteus*) was not simply a practical accessory, to hold the loincloth or over the tunic; it was formerly a symbol of virility among the peoples of central Italy, so much so that we sometimes see, on funeral paintings, warriors wearing nothing save a substantial bronze belt around the waist. Other frescoes show that belts were often trophies taken from a vanquished enemy, fixed and exhibited at the top of the spear. This early bronze belt is well known in archaeology. In the 4th century BC, it was secured with long decorated hooks. All gladiators gradually adopted this metallic *balteus*, which endured under the Principate, as a legacy from the early *Samnites*. Perhaps to better protect the belly, in the 1st century BC the closure was moved to the back, using criss-crossed leather laces, or a pin buckle. A very clear image is visible on the Fiano Romano relief. Engraved or embossed decorations generally embellished such belts.

It is not certain that these bronze belts were systematically used by gladiators outside Italy; a leather belt may have been sufficient for some. *Andabatae*, who cannot be considered true gladiators, surely did not have this traditional belt. It was also worn by gladiators equipped with a breastplate, such as *equites*.

Some documents from the end of our period state that gladiators wore a padded balaclava-style **hood** under the helmet. In leather or canvas, this hood gave more comfort, but also more protection, because it absorbed shock waves and offered some protection against head injuries. We have clear representations of gladiators wearing such hoods on the Fiano Romano relief; we also see it on the depictions of soldiers painted on the walls of Pompeii.

It is also important to discuss gladiator **legwear**. As the Gauls traditionally wore long trousers (*bracae*), it makes sense that the first *Galli* gladiators also wore this garment. Over time, this 'ethnic' garment was no longer routinely worn, and the *Galli* abandoned it. Among the gladiators, the legs were more often wrapped in cloth bands (*fasciae*); thick leather would have been inappropriate in this case. *Fasciae* were necessary to prevent the heavy metal leg armour from slipping on the leg, and hampering the movement of the

Foot protectors made of leather are worn by a *Gallus*, at the end of the 1st century BC. Such garments were also put below the greaves, to prevent them from slipping. This depiction is held at the Antiquarium di Lucus Feroniae (see also p.9). (R. D'Amato)

foot. These bands were therefore used by *Thraeces*, *hoplomachi* and even *provocatores*. In later depictions, they were also worn to protect the thighs.

To prevent the greaves from slipping, the gladiators wore on their ankles gaiters with a twisted leather ring, in the manner of Greek hoplites. Below these were sewn leather 'petals' that protected the front and back of the foot, as well as the ankle. A thin strap passed under the sole of each foot, to keep this protection in place. A shorter gaiter could also be worn on a leg without a greave. Strips of fabric could also be used as protective straps for the knee, calf, ankle, bicep or wrist.

On the frescoes of the tombs of Samnium and Lucania, warriors are almost always represented barefoot. Throughout their history, gladiators fought barefoot. Only the gladiators on horseback, the *equites*, are shown wearing fine leather **shoes** with a leather tongue on the front that hides the lacing. We do not know why this *armatura* was the only one that wore shoes. These shoes were a model for plebeians, and are identical to those worn by referees or musicians depicted on the bas-reliefs.

Body armour

The commemorative reliefs of the Principate, which inspired 19th-century painters, and then cinema, usually show ancient soldiers with bare arms and legs. In truth, the fighter was always seeking to protect his limbs. A hand or arm injury could prevent him from fighting, which was his primary purpose. He therefore added to his panoply pieces of leather, fabric or metal that allowed him to keep fighting for as long as possible.

Greaves (*ocreae*) had a long history before the advent of the gladiators. The Greek hoplites, abundantly represented on ceramics and bas-reliefs, almost all wear a pair of metallic greaves. The sheet metal was relatively thin to preserve its elasticity, because, to slide the leg into it, the edges of each greave had to be spread apart and then closed around the calf. These bronze greaves were therefore made to measure, and could be decorated with engraved or embossed patterns. During the Hellenistic period, it was common to keep them in place with two straps attached over them, at the knee and ankle. It is often believed that the Romans then preferred a simplified model, which only covered the front half of the leg. To hold them, it was necessary to criss-cross the knurl of leather laces, which slipped in rings attached to the edges. In fact, Greek-style greaves lasted until the time of Augustus. The Fiano Romano relief and the Tiber relief prove that the two models coexisted. The *hoplomachi*, the *Thraeces* and also the proto-*retiarii* each had a complete pair of greaves. The *provocatores*, and perhaps the *Samnites* as well, wore only one greave, on the left leg. The left leg was the one that was put forward, protruding under the shield.

That gladiators fought wearing only one greave may come as a surprise. The first to testify to this novel approach was Livy (*Ab Ur. Con.* IX.40), when writing about the Samnite warriors defeated in battle by Roman forces in 310 BC. However, the iconography of this period shows fighters with two *ocreae* (the exceptions are extremely rare). Silius Italicus (*Punicor* VIII.419) also writes that the Sabines wore only one greave, on the left, at the battle of Cannae in 216 BC (the Samnites were considered a Sabellian people). Polybius writes (*Hist.* VI.23.8) that the Roman legionaries of his time (in the 2nd century BC) also used a single greave, without specifying which leg. The later compiler Vegetius repeated the reference to a single greave, worn on the left leg, without specifying which period he is referring to (*DRM* I.20).

The practice of wearing a single greave was probably a survival (or an adaptation) of an initiation ritual, to which several Greek authors testify, about heroes who wore only one shoe. The best-known myth is that of

F **GLADIATORS AFTER THE REFORMS OF 22 BC (1)**
In 22 BC, the emperor Augustus reformed gladiatorialism in order to limit the risks to Roman social order. Gladiator gear was undergoing changes at this time, and swords and shields were getting smaller.

(1) *Thraex*, c.20 BC
At the end of the 1st century BC, the thighs of the *Thraeces* and *hoplomachi* were more systematically clad in bands of fabric, or of leather. The bronze greaves now extended beyond the knees, to protect the lower thighs. Indeed, the shield was smaller and squarer; the shield decoration shown here is copied from a bas-relief at the Museo Nazionale Romano (Rome, Italy). On his right arm he wears an armband made with criss-crossing leather bands. His weapon is the long *sica*. The crest of his helmet, very arched, ends with a griffin's head, which became a symbol of the *armatura*. The feathers are removable.

(2) *Hoplomachus*, c.20 BC
On the Fiano Romano relief, all *hoplomachi* (but also some *Thraeces*) have a large bead to weight the end of their ventral fabric band. Is this the mark of their *ludus*? In surviving depictions these strips of fabric usually have fringes at the end, or nothing at all. Here there is a bead about 4cm in diameter, possibly made of wood. His armband is made of leather bands, but they are assembled in parallel; the closure is done with a lace on the inside of the forearm. His Hellenistic helmet is copied from an artefact from the Detroit Institute of Arts (Michigan, USA); it is very similar to the helmet worn by a *hoplomachus* on the Fiano Romano relief. His heavy shield is hemispherical and bears a depiction of a gorgon's head based on a relief in the Musée lapidaire de Narbonne (France). To make the shield easier to hold in a defensive position, it rests on his upper left shoulder, but this is rather awkward and uncomfortable. This is why the *hoplomachi* equipped their shoulder with padded protection, held in place by strong bandages that surround the torso.

(3) *Sagittarius*, Lugdunum, c.20 BC
Like other gladiators visible on the shards surviving from artefacts made by the potter Chrysippus, this archer wears a loincloth that appears to be made from a typically Gallic checked fabric. The edge is frayed, to make fringes. His round helmet is a Coolus-Mannheim model, kept at the Rheinisches Landesmuseum Bonn (Germany), in use by the Roman legions at the end of the Republic; it has cheekpieces but lacks a crest, and is surrounded by a band in which are stitched feathers.

(4) *Tubicen*, c.20 BC
The musicians improvised during the fights. This one is dressed like the referee, with shoes and a braided tunic. Over it, he wears a rust-coloured cape. His instrument is a long, straight trumpet (*tuba*), about 175cm long, composed of several nested segments made of bronze decorated with silver. A cord is attached to its end. It is kept taut, tied to a finger, so that the trumpet does not come apart. The large mouthpiece gives more power to the instrument.

ABOVE LEFT
The shins of this *Thraex* are protected by Greek-type greaves, which wrap around the calf. This depiction is held at the Antiquarium di Lucus Feroniae. (R. D'Amato)

ABOVE RIGHT
In this depiction, held at the Museo nazionale d'Abruzzo, a *Gallus* wears a single greave. Note the feather in his headgear. Did such feathers serve to distinguish a category of gladiators, such as the *auctorati*, or did they denote a rank or function in gladiatorialism? We contend that these feathers were trophies that marked the victory of a gladiator, much like the tail and ears of the bull in a bullfight. (G. Habasque)

Jason, who came in one sandal to reclaim his throne. In Athens, children of good families, on the eve of becoming ephebes, did the same. This tradition was also imbued with magic, when it came to invoking the infernal deities. This was perhaps the real reason for the distinctive leg protection worn by certain warriors, and subsequently gladiators, whose close link with death will be recalled during funeral games. Thucydides writes (*Athemensis de bello Peloponensius Athemien* III.22.2) that the volunteers of Plataea each had only one (right) shoe when they launched a suicide attack against the Peleponnesians who besieged their city in 427 BC. Virgil relates that Queen Dido was also shod on one foot when she committed suicide (*En*. IV.518).

Mirmillones also wore a single leg pad on the left leg, but the form of this protection was very different. It was very short indeed, and covered only the area from the top of the ankle to the base of the calf. This height was sufficient to protect the foot that protruded beneath the shield, because the *scutum* carried by the *mirmillo* was larger than that of the *provocator*, and even more than that of the *parmati*. This style of leggings is visible in many contemporary depictions, but the Fiano Romano relief is the most precise. We can clearly see that this tubular protection is made of leather, sometimes with braided and studded straps; it is extended by the leather 'petals' covering the ankle, discussed above. These leather assemblies may have varied in colour.

In ancient images, the first gladiatorial **armbands** (*manicae*) appear only in the 1st century BC, but perhaps they were worn before that. Unlike the fighters of the 'archaic' period, all those of the 'technical' era wore a *manica* on the arm that held the weapon. This systematic adoption made it possible to discern a notable evolution of gladiatorialism. From this point, the gladiator was no longer simply the criminal condemned to death; rather, he had become a sportsman who must be spared and made profitable. By preserving the fighting arm, the organizers also reduced the chance of a duel being too quickly shortened by an injury, which could be frustrating for the audience, and therefore detrimental to the gladiators' reputation.

In the second half of the 1st century BC, gladiators used a short armband that covered only two-thirds of the forearm as well as the back of the hand. Its shape was inspired by the Greco-Roman boxing glove (*cestus*). Worn over

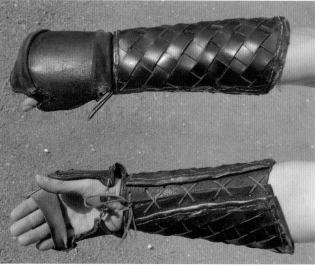

a fabric sleeve, the protruding ends of which are often visible in surviving depictions, the cuff was made of leather or sheep's wool and featured leather straps arranged in a criss-cross or in parallel, exposing the fingers and thumb. The lacing that secured the cuff was on the inside of the arm. The Fiano Romano relief shows that the *manica* worn by the *Galli* was flexible, and yet lined with scales. They could not, therefore, have been metallic, and could well have been crocodile hide, which is stronger than snakeskin.

The shape and nature of these armbands underwent changes over time, especially over their increasing length, which makes it easier to date ancient depictions. By the end of the 1st century BC, the armband had lengthened a little, and now covered the elbow. By that time articulated armbands had started to appear, made with overlapping leather cylinders; it seems that metal was not yet used to make *manicae*.

It is hard to say whether the proto-*retiarius* had **shoulder armour**. The only image we have of this gladiator is too imprecise. We believe we can guess at the presence of a curved plate on the shoulder, but without the wide edges that will exist later. This was not yet necessary, in fact, because the man has a shirt of chain mail to protect his body; such shoulder protection became more important once such gladiators shed their chain-mail shirts.

We can discern a similar type of armour worn by a *sagittarius* depicted on a ceramic of Chrysippus (see p.34). It can also be seen being worn by a *paegnarius* on an Italian bas-relief from the time of Augustus. (This last-named type of gladiator will not be discussed in this work; the first literary mention which concerns him occurs after the time period covered in this volume.) It is possible that this defence was also called *spongia*, meaning 'sponge', because the metal absorbed blows like a sponge absorbs water.

The oldest frescoes present Samnite and Lucanian warriors, whom we regard as the ancestors of gladiators, wearing different types of **breastplates**. We see the *linothorax*: a tube made from several layers of linen fabric glued together. Bands (*pteryges*) were added to protect the thighs and sometimes the upper arms. A 'U'-shaped piece was attached to the back, and the ends were folded over the shoulders and torso, for added thickness and protection. These breastplates were generally white, with painted geometric patterns.

ABOVE LEFT
Detail of a short armband, c.20 BC. Covered with scales, the material appears supple, but strong. It is possible that it is made of crocodile hide. The strap attached to the end of the sword pommel is clearly visible. This depiction is held at the Antiquarium di Lucus Feroniae. (R. D'Amato)

ABOVE RIGHT
L. Laffont's reconstruction of an armband after the Tiber relief, held at the Museo Nazionale Romano, dating from the end of the 1st century BC or the beginning of the 1st century AD. (Author's photo)

This man wears a three-disc breastplate, common among the peoples of Lucania and Samnium in the 4th century BC, and wields a *banderilla*. This depiction is held at the Museo archeologico nazionale di Paestum. (R. D'Amato)

Rarer was the bronze breastplate (*thorax*), made up of two parts. The metal was shaped to simulate the musculature of the warrior. We also sometimes see this 'muscular' armour reduced, to form plates (one on the front and one on the back) worn like a pectoral, using metal or leather straps. There are other models of pectoral, square or rectangular, and even round, but the most famous in this region of Italy was the three-disc breastplate.

We do not know whether the *Samnis* of the 3rd or 2nd century BC continued to use the breastplate, but they quite possibly did so, alongside other types of torso armour, possibly including chain mail. This latter hypothesis is based on the Mastracchio watercolour (see p.13). In his description of the Samnite fighters in 310 BC, Livy mentions a breastplate, without further clarification, but which was certainly no longer the much earlier bronze trilobed style. The pectoral, or heart protector (*cardiophylax*), also called *spongia*, was used by the Romans themselves until the reforms of Marius, at the end of the 2nd century BC, saw it replaced with a coat of mail.

During the 'technical' era, the only gladiator type who still wore a pectoral was the *provocator*. For this reason, many thought that he was the descendant of the *Samnis*, and that the *provocator* replaced the *Samnis* when the latter disappeared. This is not true, for we know of the existence of a few *Samnites* at the beginning of the Principate. It is possible, however, that the distinctions originally borne by the *Samnites* were distributed to new types of gladiator, and that the *Samnis* itself inevitably declined in popularity, hastening the type's end.

Our earliest image of this body protection is provided by the Tiber relief, dating from the turn of the 1st century BC and the 1st century AD. This depiction is interesting because it shows us the gladiators from the front and from the back, which makes it clearer how such armour was fixed. The pectoral is a rectangular plate covering the chest from the top of the ribcage to the base of the neck. Its upper edge is concave, to minimize discomfort in the throat. All the angles are slightly rounded, so as not to injure the fighter. Straps go over the shoulders or under the arms and meet at the back; where they intersect and attach to a metal disc. On the relief, the breastplate visible from the front is decorated with a gorgon's head, which was credited with the power to petrify those who looked it in the eyes. It is also found on a similar and contemporary pectoral on a relief from Dyrrachium (see p.24).

We believe that the *Samnis* still wore a breastplate in the middle of the 1st century BC, because we discern a chain mail on his panoply painted on a frieze from Pompeii. This would explain why gladiators of this type still wore the tunic a few decades later, like the *eques* when he too lost his breastplate. Before the general equipment reform was decreed, under Augustus, the *eques* was indeed protected by a *lorica squamata*, a breastplate made of bronze scales sewn onto a tunic of canvas or leather that covered part of the thighs. On the shoulders, it had two independent leather bands, which were attached to the chest and upper back. These reinforcements are clearly visible on the Glyptothek bas-relief. We do not see any hook attached to the chest to hold these shoulder pads: a piece well known to archaeology in a military context. Scale armour appeared in the Roman Army in the second half of the 1st century BC, under the influence of Eastern peoples, especially the Parthians. Therefore, if the *equites* were already well armoured in the 2nd or early 1st century BC, it must have been by employing some other type of body protection. The first image of the *equites*, discovered in the House of the Priest Amandus, is not precise enough to identify it. It appears to be white in colour. Is it a *linothorax*?

Dating from the end of the Republic, an oil-lamp depiction shows a panoply of *eques*, including a strange breastplate. The lower part appears to be made up of stitches, but above a dividing line (a waistband?), the top is hatched with vertical lines that are difficult to interpret: maybe these simply represent the long shoulder pads. The *eques* in *lorica squamata* was therefore a late invention, evident in contemporary reliefs associated with Fiano Romano, the Glyptothek (Munich, Germany) or several fragments from the Museo nazionale di Santa Maria delle Monache (Isernia, Italy), which we can date from the last two decades of the century. All these representations offer remarkable homogeneity. More stylized, the relief of the Collezione Torlonia should be viewed with caution, as the arms and legs of the gladiator are covered with scales, which could not be done in reality.

Held at the Staatliche Antikensammlungen und Glyptothek (Munich, Germany), this depiction, dating from the end of 1st century BC, shows an *eques* wearing a bronze *lorica squamata*. We see the two separate shoulder pads on the back of the gladiator on the ground. (Bibi Saint-Pol/ Wikimedia/Public Domain)

Finally, the first version of the *retiarius*, at the start of Augustus' reign, employed heavy equipment, with a helmet and leg protection but also torso armour that appears to have been chain mail or a scaled breastplate. These metallic types of armour were not worn directly on the body or the tunic; instead, they were placed on a leather or fabric garment, often padded. Called *subarmalis*, this intermediate protection absorbed shock waves to minimize the impact of violent or piercing blows. It decreased the risk of trauma, and allowed the fight to continue. It also made it more comfortable to wear the breastplate. The method of making this protective padding was also used to make armbands and hoods.

Dating from the 4th century BC, this depiction of a warrior wearing a Chalcidian helmet is held at the Museo archeologico nazionale di Paestum.
(G. Habasque)

Helmets

The oldest images, in the tombs of Paestum, reveal a well-known helmet model, now classified as the Chalcidian. Between the 5th and 3rd centuries BC, it was very widely distributed in Campania and in the bordering regions, in particular among the Samnites and the Lucanians who composed the first *armatura*. Fashioned from a piece of bronze extended by a fairly low vertical neck cover, it was fitted with two cheekpieces, generally removable using hinges. Between the neck cover and these cheekpieces, a space was cleared for the ears, the better to hear the noises of the fight and the vocal or musical commands. On this model of helmet, it was common for the front part to be stamped to form a kind of pointed visor. This decoration enjoyed a great longevity among gladiators, as among the Roman military. This helmet was sometimes surmounted by a longitudinal crest, decorated with feathers or horsehair. In addition, among the *Samnites*, cylindrical bronze tubes (or formed of a wire twisted like a spring) were frequently attached to the sides or front, to display two, four or five large feathers. We also sometimes find wings attached, made out of bronze sheets.

Pilos (conical) and Phrygian (in the shape of a Phrygian cap) helmets are much rarer, and in the latter case, only appear in Lucania. Other helmet models could also have been used by the first gladiators, such as the Montefortino type, of Gallic origin. This was very widely used in the Italic armies between the 4th and 2nd centuries BC. Around the 3rd century BC, the Attic style of helmet appeared in Italy, but we do not have an image of gladiators wearing this helmet, except in a version adapted to the end of the Republic and the beginning of the Principate.

The few depictions illustrating the funeral fights of Gauls represent them as being bareheaded. It is true that Gallic warriors made little use of helmets, except among the nobles. Even then, it was not systematic, as helmets are rarely found in Gallic graves. The Amiternum relief (if we interpret it to depict a ritual duel between Gallic chieftains) shows no helmet, while the fighters wear torso and leg protection.

G GLADIATORS AFTER THE REFORMS OF 22 BC (2)

Towards the end of the 1st century BC, and especially after Augustus' reforms, the images of gladiators become more numerous, because they were also used for imperial propaganda. The equipment of the gladiators is therefore better known to us from that time.

(1) *Gallus*, c.20 BC

This gladiator is reconstructed from a lead figurine (see p.20) from the British Museum (London, UK), shards of pottery from Lyon as well as the Fiano Romano relief. He is a provincial gladiator, wearing a checked loincloth. His helmet is a military model, with a lower neck cover; the original was discovered in a Gallic auxiliary tomb in Verdun (Slovenia), dated c.30 BC. His shield is oval and flat, with a Celtic 'winged' *umbo*. His sword is the Mainz model. He wears small leather gaiters. Clearly visible on the Fiano Romano relief, his *manica* is made from crocodile hide.

(2) *Provocator*, c.10 BC

This character is copied from the Tiber relief held at the Museo Nazionale Romano. His helmet mixes certain characteristics of the new military helmets, in particular the cutout around the ears, and the undulations of the neck cover. He wears a pectoral for protection, especially against blows from his opponent's shield, which is used in a very aggressive manner. It is held by straps that cross at the back; the gorgon's head was a common decoration. The shield (*parma*) is smaller than that of the *mirmillo*. A single greave is worn on the left leg. The sword is the Mainz type.

(3) *Eques*, c.10 BC

At the start of Augustus's reign (27 BC), the equipment of the *eques* became standardized; he now wore a metallic scale breastplate, with two narrow leather shoulder pads. It was a new model at that time, stemming from Rome's Eastern wars. The decoration of the belt is visible on a bas-relief (see p.47) in the Glyptothek (Munich, Germany). The red tunic is copied from a frieze of weapons, from Pompeii. He is the only gladiator who wears shoes, identical to those of the referees. He fights with the spear or javelins, and then continues fighting on the ground with his sword. The diameter of his *parma equestris* has shrunk. Its decoration, like the two feathers of its helmets, is inspired by a bas-relief from the Collezione Torlonia. The harness of his horse is the pattern in use at this time.

As we do not know when the *Thraex* first appeared, it is difficult to describe the first equipment employed by gladiators of that *armatura*; however, images from the end of the 1st century BC show helmets in the shape of a Phrygian cap. This is the case on one of the Campana (Italy) plaques, and some oil lamps. This model of helmet was formerly used in the Hellenistic armies, in particular by Macedonian forces, but it also occasionally appears on Etruscan funeral urns. A frieze of arms painted in Pompeii and dating from the second half of the 1st century BC shows a Phrygian-style headdress amid other pieces of gladiators' equipment, but without cheekpieces; it is coloured red and its base appears to be covered in sheepskin. The Phrygian metal helmet was very common in the Balkan regions, and in particular in Thrace. At the end of the 1st century BC, a *protome* of a griffin was added at the end of the crest; this griffin head was not yet systematic, however. The ceramics of Chrysippus, and other pieces of evidence, do not show this. Phrygian and Attic helmets were therefore worn by *Thraeces* at the end of the Republic. Although the former type disappeared under Augustus, the latter type continued to evolve, to form the helmet that we know from the excavations of Pompeii.

For the first time, helmets were specially made for the gladiatorial show. Five artefacts retrieved in excellent condition allow us better to understand the Attic helmet worn by gladiators during the 1st century BC. For example, a helmet now held at the Detroit Institute of Arts (Michigan, USA) has a profile very similar to that seen carved on an Etruscan stele from Volterra (Italy), dated *c*.80–70 BC. It is undoubtedly an Attic model, with Boeotian influence; this hybrid style is termed Attico-Boeotian. The Boeotian helmet is a headgear that offers the wearer a good field of vision. On an ogival shell, devoid of cheekpieces, it has a wide peripheral flange inclined downwards, which deflects the opponent's blows; in addition, it is stiffened on the sides by a double flute, which can also be found on later gladiator helmets. The provenance of the artefact is unknown, but it can certainly be dated to the second half of the 1st century BC. It is surmounted by a tall bronze crest, simulating a plume of horsehair. The crest is hollow to add feathers or horsehair; it ends in a long tail that protrudes from the wide neck cover. This detail can be seen on another contemporary gladiator helmet. The crest

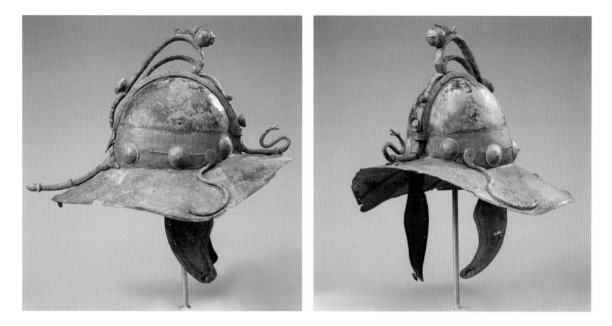

is hollow to add feathers. Its base is decorated with a faun's head, and the top with a griffin's head. The latter probably makes this artefact a *Thraex* helmet, before its form was codified further.

Unearthed in Orvieto, Italy, a second helmet is on display today at the Higgins Armory Museum (Worcester, Massachusetts, USA). Its general shape is very similar, but its decoration is a little more exuberant. This helmet also has a small lion's head on the front of the crest, with a human figure on the forehead. We find the same shape of a sheet-metal crest, but it is hollow, allowing the insertion of a piece of wood in which feathers and/or horsehair have been planted, giving the helmet a formidable height. Here too, at the rear, protrudes a metal tail, which ends in a moulding. The collar is still very wide, but it does not have the Boeotian shape described above, with its characteristic undulations that stiffen it, like corrugated-iron sheeting; a number of reinforcement bars have been added. The cheekpieces have been lost.

Preserved at the Royal Ontario Museum (Toronto, Canada), a third helmet is the most spectacular. Its data sheet states that it was discovered in the 19th century in the Colosseum, but that claim is doubtful. It has a shape very close to the previous helmet described above, but it is embellished with an extraordinary openwork crest, which is exceptional on Roman helmets in general. It has added decorative elements, especially on the front of the crest. It sports a long tail that also falls over the front of the helmet, and unfolds in the shape of a swan's neck, with an open beak. The collar is also very wide, reinforced by riveted 'S'-shaped bars. The base of the bowl is surrounded by a headband decorated at regular intervals with hemispheres, similar to those seen on the sides of the previous helmet. Perforated around their entire perimeter to sew an internal padding, the long cheekpieces have survived; at the bottom of each, a prominent button allows them to be tied with a leather lace.

A simpler Hellenistic helmet, devoid of a crest, is held at the Museum für Kunst und Gewerbe Hamburg (Germany). Frequently depicted in ancient iconography, this model may have been worn by a soldier or a gladiator.

Two views of a gladiator's helmet with an openwork crest. (Courtesy of the Royal Ontario Museum © ROM)

This Attico-Boeotian helmet was discovered in southern Italy. It is now held at the Museum für Kunst und Gewerbe Hamburg (Germany). (Author's drawing)

Finally, the helmet held at the Museo archeologico di Terni (Italy) is arguably the most recent helmet in this series. Its cheekpieces are lost, however. The large tin crest, rather crudely decorated, points us towards a *mirmillo* helmet.

We see the Hellenistic helmets depicted on the Fiano Romano relief. That of the kneeling *hoplomachus* very closely resembles the Detroit example, with its *trompe-l'oeil* crest that ends in a tail overhanging the nape of the neck. They are still present on remains from Lyon, on a *hoplomachus*, perhaps a *retiarius* and a *Thraex*. The last of these has no crest; nor does the helmet of one of the Fiano Romano relief's *Thraeces*. This indicates that the griffin's head was not yet systematic at this time. The most beautiful sculpted representations of Attico-Boeotian helmets can be admired on the Glyptothek *equites* and finds held at the Szépművészeti Múzeum (Budapest, Hungary). The wavy collar typical of this Attico-Boeotian model is clearly visible. The brace-shaped frontal decoration is very prominent on these models, and it would continue on the later generation. A relief (see p.22) held in the Museo del Sannio (Benevento, Italy) shows a *mirmillo* decked out in a simpler Attico-Boeotian helmet. Finally, let us cite two terracotta statuettes from the Museo Archeologico Nazionale di Napoli (Italy), depicting two *Thraeces*.

Probably appearing at the dawn of the 'technical' era in the second quarter of the 1st century BC, *provocatores* may have worn a Hellenistic helmet at first, like most other gladiators, but the absence of evidence

This depiction of the helmeted head of an *eques* is held at the Szépművészeti Múzeum (Budapest, Hungary). His helmet is similar to the Hamburg artefact. (S. Lagrange)

prevents us from confirming it. The first images, dated half a century later, show these gladiators wearing a different helmet, largely borrowed from Celtic tradition. Heir to an iron helmet that appeared in Gaul at the time of the Conquest – the Port type, first used by the auxiliaries of the Roman Army – it was then adopted by the legions at the beginning of the reign of Augustus in 27 BC, and improved as the Weisenau type. Its ingenious design makes it a particularly successful and efficient helmet. The Tiber relief clearly shows us two *provocatores* who wear this model of helmet. The neck cover is relatively short, but there is an embossing at its base to stiffen it, as well as a characteristic cutout around the ears. In truth, we should rather see a mixture of Gallic and Hellenistic helmets, with its accolade decoration stamped on the forehead. It was a model specially designed for gladiators.

Also of Gallic origin, a military helmet known as the Coolus type could also have been used by gladiators for a time: it is visible on a fragment of relief at the Museo nazionale di Santa Maria delle Monache (Isernia, Italy). This helmet was a simple bronze bowl, with a very short neck cover. Cheekpieces were often small rings to hang on a leather chinstrap, but they could also be metal plates notched at the eyes and mouth.

This inventory shows that gladiator equipment was not yet highly regulated. Different models of helmets were used by gladiators, and it is likely that the importance and the good fortune of some barracks allowed them to obtain the most spectacular models, which added to their reputation. Gladiators in small and poor establishments would have had to make do with simpler weapons, perhaps salvaged military equipment.

Well-known from the findings of the Pompeii barracks, the first helmets with visors appear at the end of the reign of Augustus and the beginning of the reign of Tiberius (r. AD 14–37). Their adoption is undoubtedly the consequence of the decrease in the size of swords and shields, which forced gladiators to expose themselves more while fighting hand-to-hand. However, a closed helmet was probably already being used at the end of

ABOVE LEFT
This *mirmillo* helmet, dating from the end of the 1st century BC or the beginning of the 1st century AD, is held at the Museo d'Antichità "J.J. Winckelmann" (Trieste, Italy). (R. D'Amato)

ABOVE RIGHT
A view of a *provocator* pectoral and helmet, held at the Museo Nazionale Romano, Terme di Diocleziano. (G. Habasque)

the 1st century BC. It represented the stylized features of a human face. Known as the 'sport helmet', this original model began to be used in parallel by the Roman Army's cavalry. It was used in warfare, but also during the spectacular equestrian competitions called *hippika gymnasia*.

The first military examples consisted of a simple mask, plated on the face and attached to the helmet by a front hinge, and then blocked by the folded cheekpieces. By contrast, the model worn by gladiators appears to have been of a different conception: the mask is larger, and covers the entire face down to the ears. Its originality lies in the fact that it consists of two symmetrical halves. This is how the later models 'Chieti' and 'Pompei' were also designed in the 1st century AD. Military masks never took this form.

A stele from Dyrrachium, dated to the time of Augustus, shows an *essedarius* wearing such a helmet with a face plate. Its existence is reinforced by another sculpture discovered in 1856, preserved today at the Musée Vivant-Denon (Chalon-sur-Saône, France). It depicts a *Thraex* (identifiable by his *sica*) being struck down by a lion. The presence of a scarf loincloth proves that this monument is contemporary with the Dyrrachium stele. The face helmet is very clearly sculpted, decorated with stamped animals and incised lines. A vertical centre line divides the visor into two, following the line of the nose. The top of the helmet is trimmed with decoration in the form of curly hair. The Dyrrachium stele suggests the addition of a real wig, surrounded by a headband tied at the back. Thanks to archaeology, we know many military 'sports helmets' were furnished with braided and glued horsehair.

A 'sport helmet' was very suitable for an *essedarius*, as this *armatura* fought using swords with no points; such gladiators therefore fenced only with cuts, mainly aimed at the opponent's head and shoulders. Increased facial protection would therefore make sense. This first model of fully closed helmet is very rare, but it is also difficult to identify it on the bas-reliefs of the 1st century BC. Indeed, a sculpted human face can be a real face, or a mask that simulates a face. This model still appears exceptionally in images during the Principate.

A *Thraex* wearing a helmet with a decorated mask is slain by a lion. The curly hair is arguably a braided wig. The median separation of the visor is clearly visible, as well as its embossed decoration. Now held at the Musée Vivant-Denon. (Author's photos)

Shields

All gladiators had a shield for protection except the proto-*retiarius*, who did not have a free hand to hold a shield; instead, he had protection for his left shoulder, which compensated for this lack. The size of the shield used was different according to the gladiator's *armatura*, and influenced the rest of their equipment, in particular the clothing and armour worn on the legs. In this section, we discuss wooden shields first, followed by leather and then metal shields.

Originally, the frescoes in the tombs of Paestum reveal warriors equipped with the *clipeus*, that is to say the large round and lenticular shield. It was made of wood, and could be covered with a sheet of bronze or cowhide. The user slid his left forearm inside a bronze cuff (*porpax*), positioned slightly off-centre on the inner edge of the shield. The left hand grasped a handle of braided rope (*antilabe*), attached to the edge of the shield. This shield of 1m diameter, which the Greeks called the *aspis* (or the *hoplon*), weighed about 10kg and confined the arm. It was therefore unwieldy, but it was an effective means of defence in phalanx battles, when used alongside those of other hoplites. The Campanian, Samnite and Lucanian paintings also show round models (much more rarely oval), but undoubtedly lighter, to enable the bearers of such shields to fight in a more agile fashion. Confronted with this new style of warfare, the Romans abandoned the phalanx in the 4th century BC and moved to a more adaptable and mobile army, the new manipular legion.

Besides the heavy *clipei*, round shields, lighter and covered with leather, were also used by the first gladiators. This style of shield can be seen in particular on the chariot depiction held at Paestum (see p.4): we can see the folds of the leather covering, probably stretched over a wicker frame. Such shields were named *scuta*, meaning that they were lined with skins (Festus, *De verb. signif.*: *scrautum*). The assumption that such shields were an invention of the Samnites is certainly mistaken, as they also existed among the Etruscans. This theory stems from Livy's description of the Samnites' equipment, in which he asserts that the *scuta* of *Samnites* (in his day no doubt – that is, at the end of the 1st century BC) were wider at the top than at the bottom, to better protect the upper body. This shield style is nowhere to be found in surviving depictions, however. Unfortunately, the *Samnis* as a gladiator *armatura* was disappearing as the gladiator iconography began to flourish, which also explains its absence from later sources. From this testimony, we can still postulate a slender shape for the *scutum* of the *Samnis*. A fragment of a commemorative monument found in Estepa (Spain), dating from the civil war between Caesar and Pompey (45 BC), can possibly be related to this text. Indeed, two Roman legionaries are represented with a long shield with flared edges, consistent with Livy's description. It is possible that we have here a representation of soldiers recruited from the Samnium, and equipped with their national shield. On the Estepa relief, we can make out a long vertical ridge in the middle of the *scutum*, with a protuberance in the centre. This *spina* is typical of the shields of the time of the Republic, in military usage, but also among gladiators, among whom it continued in use for another one or two centuries. At the end of our period, it was sometimes reinforced with a metal *umbo*.

Unearthed in the desert region of Fayum (Egypt), an exceptional Roman *scutum* reveals the secrets of its design. It measures 128×63.5cm. The *spina* is cut into three parts. The central one is recessed to accommodate the hand that holds the horizontal handle attached to the inside of the shield. It was made using the plywood technique, in three layers of thin wooden slats. They are curved, to better envelop the fighter, and superimposed perpendicularly. The shield's surface was originally covered with stitched felt (or leather). The rim is thinner than the middle part, which increases its lightness and flexibility, and prevents it from breaking too easily. For this type of shield, we also know examples of spindle-shaped metallic *umbones*, which flatten out against the centre of the *spina*, but images of gladiators suggest that the metallic *umbo* was little used in amphitheatres. A border made of nailed bronze segments adorns the perimeter of the shield, to prevent it from being split with a sword. It could also be made of leather, sewn, and decorated with painted or engraved patterns. Use of this infantryman's large *scutum* was revived by the *essedarii*, at least from the middle of the 1st century BC, most certainly when they abandoned their chariots to fight only on foot. Before that date, it is likely that the *essedarii* carried an oval, flat Gallic shield, more manoeuvrable on a moving chariot. It would be logical if we admit their kinship with the *Galli*. The curved shield was especially suitable for infantrymen.

Provocatores also used a *scutum*, but smaller in size. This is why we speak rather in their case of a *parma* (CIL 4.2483). It is in fact an oval *scutum*, both ends of which have been truncated, to make it lighter.

Originally, the *mirmillo* may also have carried the large *scutum* with truncated ends, and convex edges. On their oldest representations, this results in an indefinable shape, which could sometimes be called hexagonal. The *mirmillo*, however, is best known for his semi-cylindrical *scutum*, which this type of gladiator would keep until the end of the Principate. This was undoubtedly the origin of the shield of the legionary, in the form of a rectangular tile, which it must have preceded by a few decades. This shield style in the hands of Roman soldiers appears for the first time on the mausoleum of Plancus in Gaeta (Italy), *c.*20 BC. This paternity is also

---

H **THE LAST GLADIATORS OF THE 1ST CENTURY BC**

These last gladiators of the 1st century BC inaugurate different duels, because military swords were abandoned and replaced by daggers. The weapons were now very short (for most fighters), and the clashes were at close quarters.

(1) *Mirmillo, c.*10 BC–AD 10

Like all gladiators, this man wears bandages around certain limbs. The leather elements are patterned with perforations; this detail can be seen on the Fiano Romano relief kept at the Antiquarium di Lucus Feroniae (Capena, Italy). Preserved at the Museo archeologico di Terni (Italy), his helmet is an evolution from previous styles: the brim is no longer wavy and the large angular crest suggests that it belongs to a *mirmillo*. The length of swords decreased sharply at this time; they were now daggers, which necessitated a closer combat. The shield has also been reduced in size, its side edges having been cut to make it lighter. The *spina* is reinforced with a metallic *umbo*. The decoration, very military, is visible on a surviving relief.

(2) *Samnis, c.*10 BC–AD 10

This is perhaps the last version of the *Samnis*, reconstructed from a bas-relief from Nesce (Italy). His panoply is different from other known *armaturae*. He is wearing a tunic, possibly because he does not have a breastplate; the *eques* soon made the same transition. His shield is in the form of a *pelta* and corresponds to Livy's description, being wider at the top than at the bottom; this shape is often visible on the friezes of weapons. Its decoration comes from a bas-relief from the Musée lapidaire de Narbonne. His dagger precludes the possibility of identifying him as a *Thraex*. His spectacular helmet is based upon one kept at the Royal Ontario Museum (Toronto, Canada). The bas-relief is broken, however, and we do not know for certain whether this gladiator wore one or more greaves.

(3) *Essedarius, c.*10 BC–AD 10

This gladiator is reproduced from a bas-relief in the Narodni muzej Srbije (Belgrade, Serbia). The decoration of his bronze belt is inspired by a contemporary statue of a *Thraex* at the Musée Vivant-Denon (Chalon-sur-Saône, France). In these two ancient depictions, the two gladiators wear a helmet with a mask, in the style of the Roman Army's cavalry; unlike the cavalry mask, the gladiator's mask is in two parts. Our painting mixes the details of the two sculptures. This helmet has a wig, held in place by a headband. His armband protects his elbow. His sword lacks a point, which prohibits thrusting. His shield is a military-style curved *scutum*; its red colour is visible on a frieze from Pompeii.

suggested by Festus (*De verb. signif.*), who terms it *myrmillonicum scutum*. This shield measured 100–110cm in height and 70–80cm in width.

The original shield carried by the *Thraex* is unknown. On the bas-relief held at the Museo Stefano Bardini, dating from the middle of the 1st century BC, the *Thraex*'s shield appears rectangular and slightly curved, with dimensions of approximately 70×60cm. Three decades later, its shape was square and more curved; its dimensions were then approximately 60×60cm. This large *parma* can be observed on the goblet of Chrysippus and the Fiano Romano relief. By the end of the 1st century BC, they measured about 50×50cm, when the adoption of the helmet visor reduced the need for a larger shield to protect the face. This *parma* had a *spina*, and later a semi-spherical *umbo*, more generally. The *spina* and *umbo* served as much to protect the hand as they did to strike the opponent to destabilize him.

A leather shield known as the *parma equestris* was used by the *equites*. In the middle of the 2nd century BC, Polybius gave a detailed description of this shield type, but he writes that in his time the Roman Army no longer used it, due to its marginal effectiveness. Even so, it remained an element of officers' dress as a symbol of their knightly rank:

> The shields of the horsemen were made of ox skin, and had the same shape as those swollen cakes which are used for sacrifices. Not withstanding shocks, they were useless for loads and, when the rain had softened and damaged the leather, these weapons, which already were hardly useful, then became totally unusable. This is why, having observed through experience that their riders were ill-equipped, the Romans soon adopted Greek-style weaponry. (Polybius, *Hist.* VI.25.7–8)

About 60cm in diameter, the *parma equestris* was therefore made entirely of leather, on a press no doubt, and without any wood reinforcement, which explains its structural fragility. Such shields are easy to spot in the iconography, so recognizable is their singular shape, with a central protuberance surrounded by a concentric bulge. To confuse it with other models of circular shields, such as those of the *hoplomachi*, is therefore impossible. Later depictions show the inside of this shield, with a central handle hidden in the protrusion, like under an *umbo*; but this leather protuberance cannot have been effective, from an offensive or a defensive standpoint. It was while holding this grip that the rider was required to manoeuvre the reins to steer his horse, and with the other hand he wields his spear or throws his javelins. Like all shields, the *parma equestris* had painted decoration.

The shield of the *hoplomachi* was certainly made of metal, as its semi-spherical shape is difficult – but not impossible – to reproduce in wood without giving it too much thickness. Originally, it could have been made like a *hoplon*, with a wooden structure covered in bronze. Our first images of a *hoplomachus* shield, on the bas-relief held at the Museo Stefano Bardini, and on the frieze of arms painted in Pompeii, still show a shield of significant proportions (approximately 80–90cm in diameter), which underlines its affiliation with the large Greek or

A depiction of the *parma equestris*, held at the Musée départemental Arles antique (France). It would be time-consuming to describe all the designs painted on the shields, but here we will give some major types. During the first centuries of gladiatorialism, the decorative motifs were those of the 'ethnic' participants. At the end of the Republic and the beginning of the Principate, we mainly find geometric patterns, like those found on the shields of soldiers at the same time, but sometimes embellished with more figurative elements, such as flowers, palm leaves or gorgon heads. Only one surviving depiction features a model with outstretched wings typical of legionary *scuta*. Often the shield was devoid of any decoration and had a monochrome background, usually white. This last colour is most seen on gladiators, in their clothes and plumes as well. (Author's photo)

Italic *hoplon*. A quarter of a century later, its diameter was reduced to approximately 60cm (visible on a Campana plaque in particular), and at the end of the 1st century BC, it was approximately 50cm in diameter. During this evolution, its lenticular shape became markedly semi-spherical, which made it a difficult object to handle.

Because of its shape, and probably also its weight, the shield could not be held by a central handle. This was unlike other gladiator shields, which thus allowed the user to reach out to strike his opponent. A relief from the Museo Nazionale Romano and dating from the end of the 1st century BC shows a *hoplomachus* making such a strike, but this is the only image in our *corpus*. In all the other depictions, the shield is held like an *aspis*, with the arm enclosed in a bracelet, and the hand grasping an *antilabe*. The forearm is trapped inside the shield. This position forces the *hoplomachus* to hold his sword in the same hand as the *antilabe*, which is restrictive. In later images, we often see the sword blade protruding from the edge of the shield. This handicap restores the balance against the *hoplomachus*' opponents, who had only one offensive weapon.

Like a *hoplon*, the hollow of the *parma* was intended to rest on the gladiator's shoulder, to alleviate its weight – but this also caused discomfort. This is why the *hoplomachi* attached a pad between the edge of the *parma* and the shoulder. This pad was held in place by several bands of fabric or leather that enclosed the gladiator's torso; an arrangement clearly visible on the Fiano Romano relief, and on a relief at Benevento in Italy (see p.6).

Weapons

Until the time of 'technical' gladiatorialism, the weapons were those of different ethnicities, such as the great Gallic *latte* for the *Galli*. They were therefore weapons of war, and so it was until the beginning of the Principate.

Spears and javelins were the first weapons used by proto-gladiators, more frequently than the sword. It is difficult to determine a typology of the spears, because surviving points are rare and the iconography imprecise. On many grave paintings, pole weapons are handled by their ends, which are sometimes weighted, for ease of handling (see p.46). They are used in the manner of bullfighting *banderillas*, that is, by pricking them into the body of the opponent. This way of holding these weapons by their ends is still visible in representations of *hoplomachi* from the end of the Republic and the beginning of the Principate. This could suggest a filiation between *Samnites* and *hoplomachi*. If these *banderillas* are similar to javelins or short spears, they look different in the middle of the 1st century BC. Indeed, the Mastracchio watercolour (see p.13) shows entirely metal handles, with their rectangular shape achieved by bending the iron rod. This handle suggests use for thrusting, and not throwing. Such a weapon is also visible on a carved arms frieze from Pula (Croatia).

In the 1st century BC, the sword became standardized when gladiators adopted the military sword. It was initially the *gladius Hispaniensis* model, originally borrowed from the Iberian warriors of Spain. This sword was 80–90cm long overall, with a double-edged blade and a very sharp point. In the last third of the 1st century BC, weapon reforms led to a shortening of the sword, which now measured 60–70cm. The edges of the blade were lanceolate (with symmetrical wavy edges). This model is termed the Mainz sword by modern commentators. While soldiers used it until the middle of the 1st century AD, gladiators abandoned it earlier, eventually adopting an even shorter weapon. The Mainz sword is readily identifiable on many bas-reliefs. The handles are generally of the Roman type, that is, with a thick guard and an ovoid pommel, sometimes carved. A leather strap connected the sword to the fighter's wrist, preventing him from losing it.

Some *armaturae* wielded different swords. The best known is that of the *Thraeces*, which was characterized by a curved blade; the Romans called it the *sica*, or *falx supina*, literally 'false facing upwards' (Juvenal, *Sat.* VIII.201). This

A *sica* of the type wielded by the *Thraeces*, carved on the Fiano Romano relief. This depiction is held at the Antiquarium di Lucus Feroniae. This weapon was based upon the national Thracian weapon, a scythe known as the *romphaia*. It is likely that at the beginning of the *armatura*, the *Thraeces* fought with the *romphaia*. On our earliest gladiatorial images, dating from the second half of the 1st century BC, the *sica* is the same length as the Mainz swords. In this relief, we discern a double gutter on the blade, to lighten it, but also the bevel of the two cutting edges; there is also a point that emerges on the back of the blade. We find it on other representations of *Thraeces*, notably on oil lamps from the beginning of the Principate. Sometimes this point is preceded by a notch in the blade, creating the shape of a harpoon. This peculiarity, perhaps borrowed from the swords carved on some taurobolic altars, does not seem to have existed for long. (R. D'Amato)

60

blade's pronounced curvature allowed it to bypass the opponent's shield to strike his back or shoulder, or even his leg. On the relief of the Collezione Torlonia representing a hunt (see p.7), a *Thraex* fights a panther. On this occasion, he has replaced his *sica* with a straight sword, because the opponent has no shield.

If, as we assume, the *essedarius* is a variant of the chariot-mounted *Gallus*, his sword is logically heir to the long Celtic swords of the early *Galli*. Some Celtic swords had no tip, which prevented them from being used for thrusting. This fencing was not that of the Romans, who favoured the use of the point of the sword. Also, fencing only with the edges offered an original – and more brutal – spectacle, and that is undoubtedly what made it appeal to Roman audiences. *Essedarii* were therefore equipped with a straight sword, the point of which had been removed. Such a weapon is visible on the Dyrrachium stele, thus proving its early existence; it is marked with two parallel grooves, which may be the lines of the two cutting edges. This sword's length lessened over time, like other swords. With this unique weapon, an *essedarius* could not deliver the final blow to the vanquished; a sharp dagger had to be provided to him for this purpose.

Representations of *retiarii* in the 1st century BC are extremely rare, making it difficult to study their weapons. They do not, however, seem to have known significant evolutions subsequently. The trident (*tridens, fuscina*) was a kind of three-pronged fork, about 1.5m long and 25cm wide. The trident's tines were usually parallel, and sometimes had triangular tips at the ends. These 'harpoons' caused cruel wounds, difficult to heal, but also prevented the trident from being withdrawn when it was planted in a shield.

If the *fuscina* is almost always represented with the *retiarius*, this is not the case with the net (*rete, iaculum*). The net was difficult to handle, requiring the learning of a technique known to fishermen, in order for it to unfold properly in the air. If he missed his mark, the *retiarius* would be brutally crippled. This is why the inventors of the *armatura* added a cord connecting the net to the trident, facilitating its recovery and reuse.

During the Principate era, we know that the *retiarius* also carried a dagger, but we do not know whether this was also the case in the 1st century BC, because the *armatura*'s equipment changed considerably afterwards.

This rare painting, held at the Museo archeologico nazionale di Paestum, shows a duel between a swordsman and a spearman. No gladiator carried a scabbard with him to store his sword. Even the *hoplomachus*, who fought with a spear, had to hold his sword in his left hand, along with his shield, a situation that was uncomfortable for him. (R. D'Amato)

Dating from the end of the 1st century BC or the beginning of the 1st century AD, this depiction shows an *essedarius* whose sword blade has no point; he can only strike with the sharp edges. This artefact is held at the Narodni muzej Srbije. (S. Lagrange)

BIBLIOGRAPHY

Adam, Anne-Marie & Rouveret, Agnès, eds (1986). *Guerre et sociétés en Italie (Ve-IVe s. avant J.-C)*. Paris: Rue d'Ulm.

Auguet, Roland (1972). *Cruelty and Civilization: The Roman Games*. London: Routledge.

Battaglia, Dario (2010). *De rebus gladiatoriis. Dal gymnasion al ludus attraverso i sepolcri*. Bergamo: Associazione Ars Dimicandi.

Beacham, R. (1999). *Spectacle Entertainments of Early Imperial Rome*. New Haven, CT: Yale University Press.

Bellier, Claire, Bozet, Nathalie, Cattelain, Pierre & Di Stazio, Vincenze (2010). *Des jeux du stade aux jeux du cirque*. Treignes: CEDARC.

Bernet, Anne (2002). *Les gladiateurs*. Paris: Tallandier.

Briquel, Dominique (1988). 'La tradition sur l'emprunt d'armes samnites par Rome', in Anne-Marie Adam & Agnès Rouveret, eds, *Guerre et sociétés en Italie (Ve-IVe s. avant J.-C.)*. Paris: Rue d'Ulm: pp. 65–86.

Brisson, Jean-Paul (2011). *Spartacus*. Paris: CNRS.

Carter, Michael (2003). 'Gladiatorial Ranking and the "SC De pretiis gladiatorium minuendis" (CIL II 6278 = ILS 5163)', *Phoenix* 57: 83–114.

Clavel-Leveque, Monique (1984). *L'Empire en jeux, espace symbolique et pratique sociale dans le monde romain*. Lyon: CNRS.

Corbeill, Anthony (1997). 'Thumbs in Ancient Rome: *Pollex* and *Index*', *Memoirs of the American Academy in Rome* 42: 1–21.

Coulston, J.C.N. (1998). 'Gladiators and soldiers: personnel and equipment in *ludus* and *castra*', *Journal of Roman Equipment Studies* 9: 1–17.

Étienne, Robert (1966). 'La naissance de l'amphithéâtre, le mot et la chose', *Révue des études latines* 43: 213–20.

Faccenna, D. (1949–50 & 1956–58). 'Rilievi gladiatori', *Bullettino Commissione Archeologica Comunale di Roma*.

Feugère, Michel (1993). *Casques antiques*. Paris: Errance.

Futrell, Alison (2001). *Blood in the Arena: The Spectacle of Roman Power*. Austin, TX: University of Texas Press.

Futrell, Alison (2006). *The Roman Games: A Sourcebook*. Malden, MA: Blackwell.

Gilbert, François (2013a). *Devenir gladiateurs: La vie quotidienne à l'école de la mort*. Lacapelle-Marival: Archéologie Vivante.

Gilbert, François (2013b). *Gladiateurs, chasseurs et condamnés: Le spectacle du sang*. Lacapelle-Marival: Archéologie Vivante.

Gilbert, François (2014a). 'Catégories et panoplies de gladiateurs', *Prétorien* 33: 37–50.

Gilbert, François (2014b). *Les gladiateurs*. Arles: Errance.

Gilbert, François (2015). 'Les gladiateurs aux petits boucliers', *Prétorien* 34: 19–31.

Gilbert, François (2020). *Les gladiateurs: Histoire et armement*. Plougastel: Historic'One.

Golvin, J.-C. (2012). *L'amphithéâtre romain et les jeux du cirque dans le monde antique*. Lacapelle-Marival: Archéologie Vivante.

Golvin, J.-C. & Landes, C. (1990). *Amphithéâtres et Gladiateurs*. Paris: CNRS.

Grant, M. (1967). *Gladiators*. London: Penguin.

Gregori, G.L. (2011). *Ludi e munera: 25 anni di riceche sugli secttacoli d'eta romana*. Milan: LED Edizioni Universitarie.

Gunderson, E. (1996). 'The Ideology of the Arena', *Classical Antiquity* 15: 113–51.

Hinard, François, ed. (1987a). *La mort: Les morts et l'au-delà dans le monde romain*. Caen: Presses universitaires de Caen.

Jacobelli, Luciana (2003). *Gladiators at Pompeii*. Todi: L'Erma di Bretschneider.

Junkelmann, Markus (2000). 'Familia Gladiatoria: The Heroes of the Amphitheatre', in E. Köhne & C. Ewigleben, eds, *Gladiators and Caesars: The Power of Spectacle in Ancient Rome*. London: British Museum Press: pp. 31–74.

Junkelmann, Markus (2008). *Das Spiel mit dem Tod: So kämpfen Roms Gladiatoren*. Mayence: Philipp von Zabern.

Köhne, E. & Ewigleben, C. (2000). *Gladiators and Caesars: The Power of Spectacle in Ancient Rome*. London: British Museum Press.

Kyle, G. (1998). *Spectacles of Death in Ancient Rome*. London & New York, NY: Routledge.

La Regina, Adriano (2001). *Sangue e Arena*. Rome: Mondadori Electa.

Lafaye, Georges (1877–1917). 'Gladiator', in *Dictionnaire des antiquités grecques et romaines, Encyclopédie Daremberg et Saglio*. Paris: Hachette.

Landes, C., Pailler, J.-M. & Domergue, C., eds (1990). *Spectacula I: Gladiateurs et amphithéâtres*. Lattes: Éditions Imago.

Lemosse, M. (1983). 'La condition ancienne des auctorati', *Revue Historique de droit français et étranger* 2: 239–41.

Lopez, Brice & Teyssier, Eric (2005). *Gladiateurs: Des sources à l'expérimentation*. Paris: Errance.

Manas, Alfonso (2013). *Gladiadores: El gran espectáculo de Roma*. Barcelona: Editorial Ariel.

Moreau, Philippe (1983). 'A propos du sénatus-consulte épigraphique de Larinum: Gladiateurs, arbitres et valets d'arène de condition sénatoriale ou équestre', *Revue des études latines* 61: 36–48.

Mosci, M.G. (1992). *Il linguaggio gladiatorio*. Bologna: Pàtron.

Nieburgh, H.L. (1970). 'Agonistics – Rituals of Conflict', *The Annals of the American Academy of Political and Social Science* 391: 56–73.

Paolucci, Fabrizio (2003). *Gladiatori i damnati dello spectacolo*. Florence: Giunti Editore.

Piganiol, André (1923). *Recherches sur les jeux romains*. Strasbourg: Publication de la Faculté des Lettres de l'Université de Strasbourg.

Prisco, Antonio (2002). *Le statut social des gladiateurs d'Auguste à Gallien*. Paris: EPHE.

Robert, Louis (1940). *Les gladiateurs dans l'Orient grec*. Paris: Champion.

Rostovtzeff, M. (1900). 'Pinnirapus Iuvenum', *Romische Mittheilungen* 15: 223–28.

Rouveret, Agnès (1988). 'Tite-Live, Histoire romaine IX, 40: La description des armées samnites ou les pièges de la symétrie', in Anne-Marie Adam & Agnès Rouveret, eds, *Guerre et sociétés en Italie (Ve-IVe s. avant J.-C.)*. Paris: Rue d'Ulm: pp. 91–120.

Sabbatini Tumolesi, P. (1980). *Gladiatorum paria: Annunci di spettacoli gladiatorii a Pompei*. Rome: Edizioni di Storia e Letteratura.

Salles, Catherine (2005). *73 av. J.-C.: Spartacus et la révolte des gladiateurs*. Brussels: Éditiones Complexe.

Shadrake, Susanna (2005). *The World of the Gladiator*. Stroud: The History Press.

Teyssier, Eric (2009). *La mort en face: Le dossier gladiateurs*. Arles: Actes Sud.

Teyssier, Eric (2011). 'Les combats de gladiateurs', in Desbat, Armnad, *et al.*, eds, *Images d'argile: Les vases gallo-romain à médaillons d'applique de la vallée du Rhône*. Gollion: Infolio: pp. 72–103.

Thuillier, Jean-Paul (1985). *Les jeux athlétiques dans la civilisation étrusque*. Paris: École Française de Rome.

Thuillier, Jean-Paul (1996). *Le sport dans la Rome antique*. Paris: Errance.

Veyne, Paul (1976). *Le pain et le cirque: Sociologie historique d'un pluralisme politique*. Paris: Seuil.

Ville, Georges (1981). *La Gladiature en Occident. Des origines à la mort de Domitien*. Rome: École Française de Rome.

Wallon, H. (1988). *Histoire de l'esclavage dans l'Antiquité*. Paris: Robert Laffont. Originally published in 1847.

Weber, C. (1983). *Panem et Circenses*. Milan: Garzant.

Wiedermann, T. (1992). *Emperors and Gladiators*. London: Routledge.

Wuilleumier, P. & Audin, A. (1952). *Les médaillons d'applique gallo-romains de la vallée du Rhône*. Paris: Les Belles Lettres.

INDEX